ately immerse the reader into the world of an under-funded hospital and the protagonist's struggle to be released.

I0418424

What is mental illness? Well, you won't find the answer in Debbie Hartung's gripping *The Factory of Maladies*. Instead, what you'll encounter is a harrowing, firsthand account of the experience of being institutionalized. The author can't answer the question, 'Why does society lock up its disturbed and suffering souls?' But she can beautifully and clearly describe what seven days in a psych ward felt like to her. Don't miss her observations and revelations! Highly recommended.

ERIC MAISEL, PH.D., AUTHOR, *THE FUTURE OF MENTAL HEALTH* AND *HUMANE HELPING*

Debbie Hartung's *The Factory of Maladies: Seven Days on a San Francisco Psych Ward* is a striking and unforgettable memoir that lingers long after the final page.

The raw emotion and vivid storytelling draw you in from the moment you begin reading, making it impossible to put down. The characters Hartung brings to life are not just people in crisis; they are profound reflections of ourselves, exposing the inner workings of our thoughts and beliefs.

This memoir is a vital exploration of the complexities surrounding mental illness and emotional distress. Hartung thoughtfully delves into the difficult yet essential topic of suicidal thoughts and how society often responds to those in need.

Through her compassionate lens, she reveals

the deep humanity within these experiences, challenging readers to confront their own biases and preconceptions.

Poignant, powerful, and necessary, *The Factory of Maladies* is a must-read for anyone seeking a deeper understanding of mental health. Hartung's bravery in telling such a profoundly human story offers us all an opportunity for reflection and empathy.

JULIANA J BRUNO, AUTHOR OF
REASONS TO LIVE, AN INTERACTIVE GUIDE TO HEALING AND OVERCOMING SUICIDAL THOUGHTS AND HOW TO HELP OTHERS SURVIVE; CONTENT CREATOR, AND HOST OF THE *I CARE ABOUT YOU* PODCAST

Debbie Hartung's memoir, *The Factory of Maladies: Seven Days on a San Francisco Psych Ward*, takes us into a world where human frailty, strength, cruelty, kindness, indifference, empathy, suffering, and survival collide. Hartung's honest and vulnerable first-person narration draws the reader into a visceral, vicarious experience of mental illness and offers a much-needed dose of insight and understanding.

KIM COLEGROVE, AUTHOR OF
MINDFULNESS FOR WARRIORS AND
WELLNESS WARRIOR STYLE

In this beautifully written memoir, Debbie Hartung provides a window into the emotions and actions of her conscious and subconscious mind while being held against her will at a psychiatric hospital. Her forthright account of the one-week stay serves as a powerful metaphor for society and the universal challenges we all face in our own lives. Debbie takes us through the tumultuous ride of emotions she experienced, from confusion, haze, and fear to trust, awareness, and clarity, all the while exploring the effects of relatable issues such as toxic relationships, manipulation, mental health, and the quest for love, joy, and balance. Reading this heartfelt book will bring you even closer to your own self-awareness and spiritual journey.

ANGELA LOMENZO, AUTHOR
OF *WISDOM OF WILDLY CREATIVE WOMEN*

In her debut memoir, *The Factory of Maladies*, Debbie Hartung shares the reality of in-patient mental health treatment in the United States medical system. Her raw and real account explores complicated family dynamics and questionable spiritual leadership while dispelling myths about mental health care. Hartung shows us what this journey feels and looks like from inside. A must-read for anyone who has ever wondered about the 'locked ward' as well as those of us who've been there who will nod along as we feel seen and heard.

NITA SWEENEY, BESTSELLING AUTHOR
OF *DEPRESSION HATES A MOVING TARGET*

The Factory of Maladies is a generous glimpse into the heart and mind of the author's chaotic, distressing week as a psychiatric inpatient.

Hartung shares her anxieties, confusion, and anger at the characters surrounding her, staff and fellow patients alike.

This book serves two crucial purposes. First, it offers the reader a feeling for persistent mental illness and humanizes anyone who's struggling. But this read is also a call to arms for the psychiatric community, a mandate to cultivate a more humane environment for those who are suffering and to recognize the individuality and humanity of each patient, regardless of presentation.

DR. JOHN DUFFY, AUTHOR OF
PARENTING THE NEW TEEN AND
RESCUING OUR SONS

Debbie builds the mystery at the memoir's core. She weaves these scenes into accounts of harrowing details of her day-to-day life, and readers may be shocked by some of the unexpected events on the ward that she recounts. An engaging firsthand account that mixes intrigue with a promise of hope in the midst of despair.

KIRKUS REVIEWS

The Factory of Maladies is a gripping, highly emotional and raw account of a week on a San Francisco, California psychiatric ward. Dark humor, descriptive narrative and dialogue immedi-

THE FACTORY OF MALADIES

SEVEN DAYS ON A SAN FRANCISCO PSYCH WARD

DEBBIE HARTUNG

CONTENTS

FOREWORD

BY DUNCAN MACLEOD, AUTHOR OF 5150: A
TRANSFER

How delighted was I when I got to read an advance copy of
Debbie Hartung's *The Factory of Maladies?* I met Debbie
many years ago at a book launch event in San Francisco.
Since then, I had no idea that she had spent time on a
psychiatric ward like I had! Reading this wonderful text, I
got the chills. It's one thing to read, re-read, and edit one's
own recounting of time spent in psychiatric care. It's quite
another to read someone else's account!

The Factory of Maladies is a healing tool. While any
reader will enjoy this well-crafted recounting of a surreal
situation, it will be particularly helpful to families, friends,
and medical staff of the people who are going through such
difficult times. It gives a remarkable insight into the inner
workings of a mind in crisis. It also gives perspective on
what it might be like for a patient when a family member or
friend is giving the right (or wrong) kind of support. Well-
meaning people who care deeply for a beloved friend or
family member have an obligation to learn what the other
person is going through so they can be a part of the healing
process and not further exacerbate the crisis. This eloquent

story, told in the first-person, teaches how to help someone to heal.

It takes so much courage to push through the stigma and fear surrounding psychiatric disorders and tell one's story. Life after the hospital is a long healing process. Ten years passed before I was able to begin writing my own tale of incarceration, hospitalization, and subsequent guilt and humiliation leading to substance abuse. I was deeply ashamed but didn't have a name for it. Recently, organizations like NAMI have begun campaigns to identify and reduce or eliminate stigma around a health condition that should be no more shameful than a broken leg. Debbie is brave. By telling her story, she is doing her part to fight the shame and stigma that can overpower a person living with mental illness. If more people understand the humanity and struggles of such a person, they can also do their part to reduce the painful social disfavor that makes it so much harder to recover.

I've mentioned the medical professionals who care for a person in crisis. This book is for them, too. It is an invaluable opportunity to see themselves reflected in the mind of a patient for whom they are responsible. The behavior of someone healing from a psychiatric condition can appear strange or inexplicable to an outsider, even a trained professional. Understanding their condition, their mindset, and the effects of hospitalization can go a long way to improving how professionals interact with suffering people in their care. Each person is not just a "case" to be managed. They are fellow humans experiencing struggles and pressures.

The Factory of Maladies is spot-on. It tells a brave story, not only for the courage it takes to heal, but for the guts it takes to fight off external guilt and humiliation. It is an honor to give words to describe the power of this book. I know it will change lives.

Bravo, Debbie! May the many readers of this book learn from your courageous tale of healing.

For Krishna

PROLOGUE

A Short Term Effect

A day without substance
A change of thought
The atmosphere rots with time
Colors that flicker in water
A short term effect
A short term effect
An echo and a stranger's hand
A short term effect
An echo and a stranger's hand
A short term effect

THE CURE

A high-pitched buzzing sound. A cell door clanging. Gurneys being wheeled down a linoleum floor. Snippets of conversation. These sounds assaulted my feverish dreams again and again that night.

This time was different, though – heavy footsteps on a tiled floor, coupled with the squish of thick-soled shoes. The sound got louder and louder until I realized it was coming towards me. I shivered and thrashed in my bed, which was damp with perspiration, and pulled a threadbare blanket up to my chin. The mattress smelled like piss, and the room was filled with the heavy, dank smell of fear mixed with sweat.

Suddenly, the door to my room flew open, and there was a flash of brilliant, white light. I squirmed as my hands tried to shield my eyes from the blazing light. I could barely make out the outline of a figure, who glowed and was lit from behind this etheric light like an image of a saint or martyr. *It must be my guardian angel coming to rescue me from this hellish world between worlds* – a nightmare from which I could not wake up.

My hopes were dashed in an instant as the angel stomped into my room and revealed herself to be a stocky, older woman with a sour face and thick, orthopedic shoes. She looked around with beady, mole-like eyes and then, satisfied, waddled out of the room. A heavy door slammed behind her.

PART 1

HAPPY HOUSE

This is the happy house
We're happy in the happy house
Oh, it's such fun, fun, fun, whoa-uh
We've come to play in the happy house
And waste a day in the happy house
It never rains, never rains
We've come to scream in the happy house
We're in a dream in the happy house
We're all quite sane-ane-ane in the happy
    house, whoa-oh
This is the happy house, we're happy here, oh
There's room for you if you say, "I do"
But don't say no or you'll have to go
We've done no wrong with our blinkers on
It's safe and calm if you sing along, oh oh
Sing along, sing along, oh oh

This is the happy house
We're happy here in the happy house
To forget ourselves and pretend all's well
There is no hell, oh oh

SIOUXSIE AND THE BANSHEES

ONE

I awoke to find myself in a beige room – thin blankets haphazardly covered my shivering body. The room was freezing; my teeth clattered, and I could see my breath in the dim light. It felt like there was a sledgehammer in my head – my frontal cortex throbbed and pounded; there was a tingling and dull ache from my neck all the way down my spine. My jaw was locked and clenched. I shook and perspired; my limbs felt heavy and sore. I had the vague sense that someone else was in the room with me.

I looked down and saw two bracelets on my wrist, which were bright blue. The first bracelet said: *Deborah Hartung, DOB* 2/21/80 and underneath this, *Jeff Chang, MD*, followed by a long sequence of numbers. It also had a date: April 7, 2016. The second bracelet had *Penicillin, Rocephin* and *Gluten* handwritten with a thick marker; the information on the bracelets was meaningless to me, a random sequence of words and numbers that only served to confuse my brain. I couldn't ignore the cluster of bruises and puncture wounds in the crook of both my arms, as well as a huge bruise on the vein of my left hand.

I turned over in my narrow bed and looked for my

belongings, but they were nowhere to be found. I saw a scrap of paper on a bedside table with names and phone numbers, and from some faraway place, I recognized my own handwriting. My shoes had vanished, and in their place, I had been issued a pair of green socks with white tread on the bottom. There was also a brown paper bag filled with travel-size toiletries.

With great effort, I heaved myself out of bed and made my way through the shadowy room and opened the door; I immediately blinked as fluorescent light flooded my eyes and burned my retinas. With the thin blanket from my bed wrapped around me, I ghosted down the hallway, guided by some unseen force. Eventually, I ended up in another beige room.

- Good morning, Deborah. That voice. I recognized it from somewhere – a flicker of recognition fluttered through me.

- I've been trying to wake you up for an hour. Your breakfast is here. You're the last one to eat.

There was not a soul in the dining room except this woman. Her badge said 'Rosa'. She pulled out an olive-green tray with a cloth over it and plastic cutlery. There was a piece of paper with my name on it and another long series of numbers; it also said, in large letters, *ALLERGY: GLUTEN*.

I had a hard time eating because my hands were shaking so badly; I was barely able to hold the fork I was given, which was large and plastic and not sharp at all– like a set of cutlery from a game of house. There was no knife in sight. Droplets of watery coffee spilled out onto my tray. When I finally opened the lid of my food, I saw scrambled eggs and stumps of crispy bacon. As I began to eat, some of the nausea I felt earlier disappeared. I realized that it had been days since my last meal. I ate bacon for the first time in twenty years, and when Rosa came around and offered me more coffee, for a split second, I thought I was at a diner. It didn't register when she said, - We only have decaf *here*.

I finished my meal and tried to steady my trembling hands as I carried the tray to Rosa. She took it from me and placed it on an empty shelf. As Rosa did this, an Asian girl who appeared to be about twenty years old walked in – she was wearing shorts and a black hoodie, her face was covered in red constellations of acne, which left tiny bits of clear skin exposed. She had small eyes that darted around the room.

- No breakfast? Rosa asked.

She shook her head. She had the air of someone who had just gotten out of bed and was groggily making her way into her own kitchen. She croaked – Caw-fee in a high-pitched voice that sounded like a five-year-old with a speech impediment.

- Caw-fee!

- Ok, Connie.

- I WAN CAW-FEE AND A CIGARETTE!

- I know, Connie.

With that, Rosa poured the coffee, which Connie snatched from her without a word of thanks; she turned on her heels and walked out of the dining room.

My head throbbed as I slowly walked back to my room. In a daze, I shuffled down the hallway. I did not seem to be able to walk properly – my feet kept sliding out from under me; the tread on the bottom of the cheap slipper socks was no match for the slick, clinical floor. I hunched over and wrapped the blanket tightly around myself in a futile attempt to keep warm. As I turned right down the L-shaped corridor, I walked past a series of rooms. The doors were open, and I could see figures curled up or sitting on unmade beds, all with vacant stares and hunched over.

Through the haze of my dream-like state, I heard a woman's voice in the distance; it seemed strained. She was calling out someone's name. Eventually, I realized she was addressing me.

- Deborah, come here. I approached a counter and found an older woman with gray hair speaking to me.

- Let me scan your wristband.

I uneasily held out a shaking hand – my wrist bone jutted out, and the blue bracelet slipped down my forearm. She grabbed the bracelet and held it in place while she scanned it with what looked like a gun from a supermarket. In response, the gun made a loud beeping sound and flashed red. The woman stood up from her chair - she moved slowly and arthritically, with a gimpy leg, and then disappeared behind a closet door.

When she emerged, she was carrying two paper cups – one with a single white pill and the other with water. I took the pill. Her rheumy, cloudy, and cataract-covered eyes focused on my throat. When she seemed satisfied that I had swallowed the pill, I was dismissed.

Routine actions took over my disconnected state, and I found myself making my bed as if I were at home. Opening the curtains proved to be difficult; all the strings and pulleys were missing. I had to push them apart with my quivering hands. Eventually, the heavy, dark fabric parted to reveal a dirty window.

A thin white towel lay on the bedside table. I peered inside the brown paper bag that I had been given and pulled out a bar of soap and a small bottle of shampoo. Dental floss, a razor, and shaving foam were markedly absent.

I went to the bathroom to undress, but the room was so small I could barely move. It reminded me of a bathroom from a cheap hotel. When I took off my scrubs, I found myself wearing my best black lace bra and a pair of disposable underwear. I shivered in the frigid air and waited for the water from the shower to heat up. As I washed myself, I noticed a damp and musty washcloth curled on a ledge; a thin bar of antiseptic soap lay on top of it.

I dried off as best I could with the rough towel, but it barely worked, and I was still wet. I hardly had enough room to get dressed, but I managed to put on my bra and the same pair of scrubs, which were damp and reeked of sweat. I avoided looking at myself in the small, fogged-over mirror as I brushed my teeth. I walked out of the bathroom and came face to face with an elderly, heavyset Latina woman with dark, greasy hair and glasses. She was putting clothing into a white plastic bag.

- I'm going home today, she said and smiled. I was incapable of any form of conversation, so I nodded my head and grunted in response.

Exhaustion overtook me, and I crawled into bed. I pulled all four blankets around myself, but I still shivered. I lay there in the fetal position and stared at the concrete wall; my blue bracelets were the only color in the room.

TWO

I found myself back in the dining room – surrounded by a sea of purple scrubs. A small and silent group was gathered around the large table – each person seemingly indistinguishable from the next, with the same glazed and bloodshot eyes that stared into outer space without focusing on anyone or anything in particular.

We were given the task of cutting out uplifting words and phrases from a sheet of paper and affixing them to a colored piece of cardstock. A very enthusiastic woman proceeded to place childproof scissors and stacks of vibrantly hued paper on the table. She called herself 'Jen' and said she was our O.T. for the day.

- Who can tell me why positive word association is so powerful? Suddenly, my mind went blank and fuzzy; I felt disconnected – a head and body acting as two separate, floating entities. Jen's voice jolted me back into the present moment.

- If you're unable to use the scissors, words and phrases are already cut out for you...

I fumbled around and grabbed a pair of scissors—they were extremely small, with dull edges; I tried in vain to hold them in my twitching hand. Eventually, I managed to glue a few phrases onto my piece of pink paper. As I looked around the room, I saw that everyone else was quietly at war with the scissors.

- Deborah, the doctor wants to meet with you. Please go back to your room.

As I stood up, I felt dizzy and unsteady. I swayed as I picked up my arts and crafts project from the table; I barely made it to my room.

A stack of papers awaited me on the bedside table. I picked up a pamphlet entitled ***Your Healing Journey*** and immediately threw it down. Next was a small, green sheet of paper with ***Visiting Hours*** written on it; I gleaned that visitors were allowed Monday through Friday, from 2-4 pm and from 7-9 pm; on the weekends, visitors were allowed from 1-8 pm. I also learned that the following items were considered unsafe and were not permitted on the 'unit': plastic bags, belts, glass, sharp items, cans, smoking materials, and alcohol.

Finally, I picked up a yellow carbon copy of an official-looking document; my hand trembled as I perused the paper. I shuddered as I saw my full name in print – it was typed out so carefully. I tried to read the rest of the document, but my eyes wouldn't focus – they were two kaleidoscopes moving in opposite directions. My heart pounded, and my chest was tight; I felt clammy as beads of sweat formed on my forehead and top lip. My mind spun; I was overcome with nausea, and the faint taste of something metallic rose in my throat. The room seemed to get smaller and smaller by the minute, and my limbs turned into useless, jelly-like appendages. I was floating far, far away, and then: darkness. A dense fog of nothingness settled upon my memory.

- DO YOU EVER HEAR VOICES?

- No.

- Do you ever have manic episodes? Times when you feel euphoric or invincible, followed by a severe low?

- No. I never seem to get the highs, just the lows...

When I came to, I found myself sitting on my bed; a man sat on the unmade bed across from me. He had a chubby, worn-out face and ears that stuck out. A large paunch extended over his trousers. According to his badge, he was Dr. Mueller, a resident psychiatrist, even though he looked to be almost fifty years old. He rapidly fired questions at me, which, to my astonishment, I felt compelled to answer. It was as if I had been given an injection of truth serum.

- What medications have you taken in the past?

- I was on Cymbalta and Xanax for fifteen years.

- Before that? This seemed more like a demand rather than a question.

- Prozac, Celexa, Paxil, and Effexor. He scribbled furiously on a piece of paper.

- Have you tried anything like this before? The words echoed in my mind, and I furiously attempted to understand what he meant; I tried asking him to repeat the question, but he had already moved on.

- How's your living situation? Would you describe it as stable?

- Yes.

- Do you live by yourself or with others?

- I live with my boyfriend. He raised his eyebrows at this information.

- There's nothing about him on your intake form, and

you didn't say anything about him when I spoke to you before.

My brain clicked and churned in a useless attempt to remember our previous conversation, but all efforts were in vain. As far as I knew, this was my first meeting with Dr. Mueller.

- And where is he? It took me a moment to remember that he was asking about Krishna, but even in my bewildered state, I felt the implication of his question.

- It's not like that...we've been together eleven years, and he...he takes care of me.

Dr. Mueller was growing impatient. – But where is he *now*?

- India. He's visiting his family.

- Can I contact him?

- No...he doesn't have a cell phone, and he's not checking his email. This was met with a dubious look and more scribbling. Finally, he changed the subject.

- Have you ever been hospitalized before? My head ached as I tried to answer his question; eventually, I was able to pull an answer out of the dark, murky void of my memory.

- Once. When I was seventeen.

- What happened?

- I don't know...I .... I think I had a nervous breakdown.

- Are you currently seeing a therapist?

- Kind of. I have...I had a spiritual teacher. He looked at me questioningly.

- Where did you meet this "teacher"?

- Through my aunt...she knows him.

- Is he local?

- No. He lives in Sedona. I have met him in person, but we were doing sessions over the phone. Dr. Mueller looked at me with utter disbelief.

- Why weren't you seeing a licensed therapist in San Francisco?

- I was, but he, Bodhi, my teacher...he...he said I didn't need to see her anymore. A tiny bit of reality pierced the veil of my bewildered state; I felt as if something invisible was choking me, and, like a caged animal, I knew I was trapped.

- I have a doctor. Dr. Gerard. Can you call her for me? I pleaded with my inquisitor.

- She's well aware of your situation. She knows you're here.

I felt tears well up in my eyes – if Dr. Gerard knew I was here – whatever this place was, why wasn't she helping me? Why wasn't she here?

- Deborah, I need to inform you that you are on a 5150, which is a legal hold. You will be here for seventy-two hours, and then we have the option to extend the hold indefinitely.

Time seemed to move in the past, present and future all at once. Worlds seemed to collide and burst; I felt like a microcosm in an explosion. The doctor's voice shocked me back into the present moment.

- Are you having thoughts of self-harm? I looked off into the distance, and I felt my heart break in half and then splinter into shards.

- No, I whispered.

The conversation with Dr. Mueller finally ended, and when he left the room (*my* room), I went over to the window. Rain came down in a steady drizzle, and because of the dark screen on the window, which was permanently sealed shut, no light could penetrate. I stared out of the dingy window and was able to make out a gray concrete building next door. Ambulance sirens constantly blared and flashed bright white and red lights; tiny cars moved up a hill. The color of the industrial building tangled with the rain to create an overall atmosphere of gloom, sadness, and despair.

THREE

- Come on, Jerome, it's time to go.

Dr. Mueller's voice was firm, but Jerome continued to ignore him; he talked and mumbled to himself, while simultaneously shoveling food into his mouth with an air of determination.

- Now, Jerome. Let's go.

- BUT, I GOT NOWHERE TA GO, MAN! Jerome screamed while crumbs flew from his mouth.

Dr. Mueller seemed unfazed and stood his ground. Clearly, he had heard this before and did not particularly care; Dr. Mueller was overworked and overtired. The dark circles under his eyes and bloated face seemed to confirm this.

Jerome stood up abruptly and nervously shifted his weight from his left to right leg; I realized his gargantuan size and height – he towered over the doctor. I also noticed that he was wearing street clothes – a dirty, hooded sweatshirt that once read 'Adidas' and baggy jeans – while the rest of us were in purple scrubs. Dr. Mueller quickly led him away; no one else at the dining room table seemed to notice.

I went back to my room; the cold seeped into my bones and my already aching joints. I crawled into bed and watched the rain pour down and silently splatter against the window. A part of me still harbored the belief that this was a dream – a simple mistake that could end instantaneously if only I could will my eyes to open. I shivered and stared at the beige walls; an overall sense of terror seemed to be creeping up on me. It settled on me like a heavy Afghan blanket, and then, all at once, I was encased by it; fear gripped ahold of me, and I was completely smothered.

MY EYES BURNED in the fluorescent light of the hallway, which was such a stark contrast to the dim lighting of my room. I wandered around aimlessly, disassociated. I found myself at the nurses' station – a ragged fingernail with overgrown cuticles pointed to a sign: *Do Not Loiter Around The Nurses' Station*. As I turned away, I heard Connie's voice.

- Is it time now? She asked excitedly, hands clapping. A stern voice boomed in response.

- NO! You just had your Nicorette. You don't get another piece for a few hours. I thought I heard Connie whimper as I shuffled down the hallway.

I found myself back at the nurses' station; for the first time, I saw a huge clock on the wall to the left of the counter. It read 2:15. I watched the hands on the clock move in slow motion, and then, suddenly, I heard a loud buzzing noise followed by the heavy slam of an iron gate. The nurse on duty was glued to a monitor on her desk, and when her eyes finally looked up from the screen, they peered, hawk-like, at a small figure walking through a swinging door.

My aunt hugged me stiffly; I felt limp in her forced embrace. My heart beat wildly with a sense of apprehension. She was tall and sporty – naturally muscular and wiry - the type of thin person who was disgusted by fat people. She wore a faded t-shirt with a Ganesha on it, a North Face jacket, and khaki cargo pants. Prayer beads and a clear quartz crystal dangled from her neck.

- You've lost weight. She stepped back and scanned me with her small, blue eyes.

- *Have you lost weight?* I didn't answer her question; I just stared at her vacantly.

- Look at your outfit! At least it's a color you like.

- You've cut off all your hair – at least it's not pink like it usually is. I was too embarrassed to admit that I had pulled out most of my hair.

I wanted to feel a sense of comfort from my aunt's presence, but it only seemed to confuse me. Seeing her instilled the concept that this wasn't a hallucination or a bad dream; the feeling of floating between worlds, touching down for a brief instant, was real. This ever-present, morbid, trance-like state was no illusion; it was reality.

FOUR

- Look at you – you're a nervous wreck.

I felt shame rising inside of me as I saw myself through the eyes of my aunt. I was curled up on a chair in the empty dining room, my heels on the bottom of the cheap, plastic seat. My arms were wrapped around my body, and I was compulsively biting and gnawing at my cuticles. I rocked back and forth. I could feel that my face was sunken and gaunt. I looked at my aunt with hollow, sad eyes and sobbed.

- What have I done? I buried my head in my hands and bawled.

- This negativity has got to stop. That's what I've been telling you all along – it's just too much, and it's the root of all your issues.

- Where am I? My aunt ignored my question.

- WHERE AM I?

- You are exactly where you need to be.

My aunt's New Age platitudes grated on my already fragile nerves; all I wanted to know was my physical location in the city.

- Please get me out of here! I begged and pleaded to no avail.

- You know, I was listening to Abraham* the other day and it gave me a lot of clarity. What's happened here is that you have had a balancing out of energy. You were so negative, for such a long period of time, and this energy had to go somewhere. It really needed to balance out. You could have either balanced this karma the graceful way, with Spirit, or the hard way. Clearly, you chose the difficult path.

I had no idea what she was talking about, but I sensed that her speech was not yet over. A sense of confusion and hopelessness washed over me.

- Look at me, I got a phone call that you were in the hospital. I then *decided* to come visit you. *Intention*. I told the goddess that I needed a place to stay and then I looked online for a hotel. I booked a hotel in Japantown because it was close. And really, who knew there was a Japantown here?! The nurse I spoke to said The Kabuki Hotel was nice. *This was confirmation from the goddess*. Then I said, 'thank you.' *Gratitude*.

She looked down at me from the tip of her nose. – That's how it's done. *That's how you manifest*.

With that, my aunt stood up and left the room. Visiting hour was over.

* Abraham-Hicks channelings

FIVE

A day had passed in the outside world, yet on the inside, time stood still. I did not sleep a wink – a cacophony of horrifying sounds, as well as the intense cold, kept me awake the entire night. A few times, my eyes sealed shut of their own accord, only to pop open when the door to my room shot open for a safety check. Eventually, the screams and yelps of the other patients subsided, and the slamming of doors gave way to the sounds of the morning: breakfast trays being delivered, wristbands being scanned, the heavy opening and closing of the medication closet and patients dragging their feet down the corridor to watch television in the Day Room.

I pushed the thin, damp blankets off of my body – they stunk of stale sweat and terror. The room was still freezing; my teeth clattered as I crawled out of bed. I saw faint wisps of my breath, like smoke curling up gently and effortlessly from the end of a cigarette in a black-and-white movie. The rain came down in a steady drizzle and created tiny droplets of film over the window, like an all–gray pointillism painting.

I showered with scalding hot water to sanitize myself.

The used washcloth and bar of Dial soap were still present, becoming increasingly moldier by the minute. As soon as I stepped out of the shower, I was engulfed by a gust of cold air.

I stood in front of the mirror, misty and wet with condensation, and brushed my teeth; coarse bristles from the travel-sized toothbrush fell into my mouth. I put my scrubs back on – they seemed to stick to me. I put on a dark blue sweatshirt, which a mysterious friend had dropped off for me; I raised the hood over my head for extra warmth and then, exhausted, went back to bed.

I lay on my bed for what seemed like an eternity. Finally, my eyelids became heavy, and sleepiness overtook me. Just as I was falling asleep, the door to my room flew open, and a voice chirped:

- Good morning, Deb-o-rah! Breakfast is being served in the dining room.

I slowly made my way down the hallway; my limbs felt like lead, and I was discombobulated. Out of nowhere, a figure clad in purple scrubs crossed my path and almost ran into me. I caught a glimpse of a Caucasian man in his late thirties with cropped white hair and white stubble on his chin; he paced up and down the corridor with a frenzied look in his bulging eyes. His focal point lay intently on something in the distance.

As soon as I entered the dining room, Rosa asked me to sit down. Immediately after doing so, she took my blood pressure and spurted out a stream of numbers to me.

- Do you take blood pressure medicine? Rosa questioned.

- No... I looked at her quizzically.

- Hmmm...your numbers are very high. Have you been under any extra stress lately?

I stared blankly at Rosa and tried in vain to ignore her utterly ridiculous question. She broke the silence.

- Have you had a bowel movement today?

My mind churned as I tried to remember. – No, but I had one last night. She was very interested in my response and scribbled notes on a sheet of paper.

I pushed the eggs around my plate; I had no appetite. The other patients gobbled their food as if they had not been fed for days. Somehow, the manners I had been taught as a child and young adult overrode the trauma I was experiencing, and I found myself behaving as if I were at a fine dining establishment. My thin, paper napkin was placed on my lap, the plastic fork was to the left of my plate, and the strange contraption that was supposedly a knife was to my right. I occasionally dabbed my mouth with my napkin.

I was slightly horrified by the table manners (or lack thereof) of the other patients. I ate slowly and barely at all while they ate everything in sight with wild volition – elbows hunkered down on the table, food flying into their gaping, open mouths like pigs at a feeding trough. My fellow patients barely chewed their food - they just swallowed. They ate every morsel in sight, and when they were done, they looked at the extra food on my tray with intense lust and envy.

After breakfast, I wandered down the hallway, my green slipper socks sliding and catching on the slick linoleum floor. I walked past what I assumed was the Day Room; I recognized many of the ghoulish faces from the dining room. They were parked on a dirty couch, with their eyes plastered to a television. It appeared that the Weather Channel was on; from a distance, I could make out rain clouds, which stretched the entire length of the screen.

- DEBORAH, come here. A nurse motioned for me to approach the front desk. I ambled toward her and looked up at the large clock on the wall – it read 9:15.

- It's time for your meds. Wait here. She hoisted herself up from her chair and headed towards the medication closet. Halfway there, she changed her mind and turned around.

- Let me scan your bracelet.

She reached for my wrist and brought out what looked like a toy from a video game I had played as a child, but I could not remember what it was called; my mind drew a blank. Time moved laterally, from the past to the present moment, in slippery movements over which I had no control. A series of loud beeps and bright red lines emanating from the scanner startled me, forcing me back into the present moment.

- Stay here.

Once again, the nurse rose from her seat and approached the medication closet. She held her badge up to a card reader, which in turn made a series of clicking sounds. She then entered a long series of numbers onto a keypad and used a key that hung from a lanyard around her neck to unlock the door. The nurse disappeared into a dark cavern, and when she finally emerged, she was holding two miniature paper cups.

A single white pill disappeared into one of the small cups; water filled the second. I swallowed the pill as the nurse stared at my mouth and throat. Just as I finished, I turned around to find Connie inches from me.

- What is it, Connie? The nurse asked with a great deal of annoyance.

- Nic-or-ette! She made this proclamation and then shuffled around the counter; she grabbed her hands together like a small child awaiting a slice of birthday cake. The nurse continued to glare at Connie.

- Not time yet. Not until lunch.

- Awwww! Connie balled her fists up and started to slink away but suddenly changed her mind.

- Can I use the phone? She slyly asked.

SIX

- Deborah, I'm Dr. Chang. I've been talking to Aurelia – your aunt, I believe? She asked me to look into transferring you to a month-long rehab facility. This would be after your discharge from this hospital, of course.

I was instantly overcome with alarm and foreboding; my heart pounded and throbbed wildly in my chest. I fixed my eyes, large with trepidation, on Dr. Chang; he continued to flip through a stack of papers with the air of an extremely busy man. He appeared to be in his mid-sixties and was very well groomed; his jet-black hair had naturally stylish gray streaks in it and was styled into a faux-hawk; he wore an expensive black cashmere sweater atop a pair of tight, mustard-colored jeans.

- This is a very unusual situation; your aunt mentioned that your family has 'resources,' but we don't usually recommend this protocol unless there has been an intense substance abuse problem.

I groaned and felt my body break out in a cold, clammy sweat. I felt that he was awaiting a response. I managed to spurt out:

- I....I'm not a drug addict. A minute passed and the doctor had not acknowledged my comment.

- My aunt is very wealthy – and very controlling. Do I have to go away?

Dr. Chang hastily scanned a piece of paper he held in his right hand; when he finally looked at me, his dark eyes bore into me with intense inquisition.

IT WAS my first time in the Day Room; I was overcome with the smell of musty, old furniture. A ratty, tan-colored couch placed in front of the television seemed to be the culprit. There was a large dining room table with six upholstered chairs, which were blue at one time. The color had faded long ago, and the chairs were dotted with dark stains and holes. Two large, locked glass doors looked out onto a concrete patio, most of which was concealed by the pounding rain.

A woman sat in a chair, facing the entrance to the Day Room. She looked heavily sedated; her hazy gaze was without a focal point, and I did not see her gray eyes blink. She silently sat there, hunched over like an old woman, yet her thick, dark brown, almost black hair shined with health and was styled in a pixie cut. Her head was cocked to the right side, and her stance reminded me of my Nana after her stroke.

Out of nowhere, she spoke: - I'm Lauren. First time? There was a kindness in her voice.

- Yeah... My voice trailed off, and I suddenly felt choked up; I could not muster any other words.

- It can be scary your first time. As Lauren spoke, her stance and gaze did not shift in the slightest, and her mouth stood still; she was a ventriloquist of sorts. Her face was young (mid-twenties), but the deep cuts, carvings, and scars on her arms and wrists betrayed her long and troubled past.

I tried to think of something to say to her, but my head pulsated with pain, and my mouth seemed to be sealed shut. We sat together in silence for what seemed like hours, joined together by the invisible thread of our mutual anguish.

SEVEN

The lights flickered on and off in the Day Room; I expected a loud thunderclap to come from outside, but the only sound I heard was the incessant rain pummeling against the window. Nonetheless, Maryanne, our Occupational Therapist for the day, seemed startled.

- Anyway...moving on. Who's next? Her question was met with a wall of stony silence and downcast eyes.

- Alex, will you share your answers with us? She gently asked.

The man I had seen pacing up and down the halls clenched his sheet of paper and looked up briefly – his eyes bulged out of his skull, and he began to compulsively stroke the bright white stubble on his chin.

- Are you willing to share your answer to one question with us? Maryanne pleaded. Alex nodded yes.

- What are three things that cause you stress?

- Job interviews. Work. Time wasting. Alex spat out his answers and crossed his arms angrily. I tried to focus on Maryanne's response, but my attention waned to my own blank questionnaire.

Worksheet – STRESS

1. *Name 3 things that cause you stress.*
2. *What are 3 signs and symptoms of stress for you?*
3. *List 3 positive things you can do to make yourself feel better.*
4. *On the back of this sheet, draw a picture of a place where you feel relaxed.*

I clenched my miniature yellow pencil and scribbled down answers to the three questions; in an ironic twist of fate, the exercise around stress caused me immense anxiety. I felt my heart pound as my sweaty grip tightened on the pencil. As I turned my paper over and attempted to draw, I thought I heard Lauren mention something about graduate school being her major stressor.

- Deborah? I looked up and saw Maryanne's hazel eyes focused on me – they were full of expectation and a little concern.

- We haven't heard from you yet. Will you please share your answers with the group?

My hands shook as I gripped my questionnaire; I felt as if a huge spotlight was cast upon me as I perspired and felt my throat tighten; there was a high-pitched ringing in my ears. I felt dizzy and befuddled.

- Deborah? Are you still with us? I managed to slowly nod my head.

- Can you share one answer with us? I blinked. Maryanne assumed this was my way of communicating 'yes.'

- Let's see your drawing. I heard you're an artist – is that right? I could not manage an answer to her question; my mouth felt like it was stuffed with a wad of cotton. I tentatively turned over my worksheet and showed Maryanne my drawing – a messy, crude attempt at my living room.

- What is that? A tree? She inquired, a little too kindly.

- It...it's my apartment. My living room has a round window. It took all my energy to sputter out this answer.

EIGHT

Aurelia slammed a notebook onto the dining room table.

- Don't waste your time in here – do something productive with yourself, she said accusingly.

I didn't bother to tell her that I was not allowed the use of pens or pencils without supervision, as they were considered sharp objects.

- I brought you something else. Aurelia pulled out a laminated photo from her jute tote bag and threw it onto the table; it looked like a female version of the Buddha. The deity was atop a pink lotus and holding a carafe; beams of orange light emanated from behind her.

- That's Quan Yin. She's my goddess, so that makes her your goddess, too. This time, her tone switched from frustration to one of forced compassion.

I looked at Aurelia with a puzzled expression, but she continued to blast me with her thoughts, ideas and intuitions regarding what she called my "situation."

- I've been thinking that what you need is structure. You've had too much free time on your hands and look where it's gotten you. You really need to get a job – do something with yourself. Volunteer. You know, there are a lot of people much worse off than you are. What you need to cultivate is an *attitude of gratitude.*

I felt dazed and foggy as the continuous throbbing in my head worsened; I tried to find the words to defend myself, but my mind was blank.

- I was working... Lucky...I was painting-

- That doesn't count. Aurelia had always disliked – and never understood - my abstract paintings.

- Who's Lucky? You've been repeating this name for days now.

- He's...he's the dog I walk. My chest felt constricted, and my anxiety rose as I thought of Lucky left waiting for his daily walks; I was being crushed by the weight of my guilt.

- Never mind. He'll be fine – he's *just a dog.* Aurelia stressed this point repeatedly, but it did nothing to assuage my guilt; in fact, it only made it worse.

- I KNOW we've been talking about structure today. I really can't stress how important it is for you to have it in your life.

I started to mumble a defensive response, but Aurelia held her hand up to silence any further interruptions.

- You can't just go home after this. You need a founda- tion, rules, and someone to be accountable to. What you need is structure, and you won't get that in your apartment.

- Krishna will be home... I interjected.

- You don't know what's going to happen with him. This might be the last straw for him; who can blame him, really? What you really need is to go to a halfway house or something.

- What?! That's for people who have just gotten out of jail.

Terror gripped every inch of my body; I pleaded to be allowed back into my apartment. I was very attached to my home, and the thought of not returning there caused my anxiety to soar. Amidst all this fear, my thoughts shifted to my parents. Internally, I cried and yelped for them like a small child; I prayed to a god I didn't believe in to contact them on my behalf and ask them to rescue me from this living hell. I began to whimper. Aurelia looked at me with icy blue eyes, and then, instantaneously, her gaze shifted to something - or someone - behind me.

Dr. Mueller sat down next to Aurelia and his hefty belly extended a good five inches over the table. He did not acknowledge me at all, yet through the briefest of nods and a moment of intense eye contact, a silent understanding flashed between Dr. Mueller and Aurelia.

A sense of déjà vu washed over me as I stared at Aurelia; I could see her mouth moving, but I could not hear her words. She looked like a marionette doll - someone from above was pulling her strings and causing her to gesticulate wildly and continuously clap her mouth open and shut with finite movements. Dr. Mueller's puppeteer must have been asleep on the job because he just sat there, unmoving, with a detached look on his face.

My heart thudded loudly in my ears as it seemed to have leaped from my chest to my throat, and my airway constricted; I compulsively scratched my skin, and my left eye twitched uncontrollably. I felt like I was hallucinating — everything around me seemed to take on a strange, surreal quality; Aurelia and Dr. Mueller morphed into terrifying creatures. I dropped in and out of my body as my mind swirled in complete and utter sensory overload.

Intermittently, I was able to hear again; phrases like

'long-term facility,' 'rehab,' and 'structure' were hammered down from above and flooded my consciousness. Yet, amidst all this turmoil, there was a spark of comprehension on my part. It took every ounce of energy I had to become lucid again and to fight for myself. I was shaking all over as the realization hit me: Aurelia and Dr. Mueller were going to lock me up and throw away the key.

- I'M AN ADULT, AND I'M NOT DOING IT! The words flew out of my mouth with intense speed and rancor.

I sat there, stupefied in the aftermath of my outcry. Dr. Mueller merely nodded his head. Aurelia turned into a petulant child – she raised her bottom lip over her teeth, which engulfed her top lip and made her wrinkles more pronounced; she crossed her arms and moved her legs nervously. From then on, she avoided all eye contact with me and spoke only to the doctor. When the meeting ended, she rose from her chair and stomped out of the room.

NINE

I kept a wide-eyed vigil from my bed that night; I was terrified that another patient would attack me the moment I drifted off to sleep. I could hear Connie, in the room next to mine, pacing back and forth, talking to herself and scratching at the walls. I shivered as I remembered her saying that "the voices" kept her awake until morning.

Every fifteen minutes, the door to my room flew open, and an extremely harsh light flooded my eyes.

- Still up? A male nurse asked me. I nodded my head 'yes'.

He quickly scanned the room and made his exit, leaving the door wide open. I felt exposed and endangered; I climbed out of bed, rushed to the door, and securely closed it before the jarring sounds of the night could scare me again.

Fifteen minutes later, the nurse returned, leaving the door wide open after he determined that I was not in imminent danger of hurting myself. Once again, I frantically shut the door.

Finally, exhausted from my hyper-vigilance, I curled up in a ball and rested my head on the pancake-thin pillow atop of my bed. I repeated my mantra of *This isn't happening* over and over again. I existed in a fragmented reality, a living purgatory, where shattered thoughts, images, and experiences invaded my consciousness at will.

Krishna. His face was all I could see, and I yearned for his gentle touch. I trembled as I saw visions of him holding me at night as we drifted off to sleep – our bodies entwined like chromosomes on a strand of DNA. Then the television set of my mind suddenly changed channels, and instantly, he was hovering somewhere in the distance, like a trusted narrator, ever-present and all-knowing. I saw him feeding me bright yellow daal. Then he was playing records; I seemed to have X-ray vision, and my eyes zoomed in on the tiny needle, finding the groove of the heavy vinyl. I heard a familiar guitar riff and a cowbell ringing as *The Passenger* filled the air. Krishna emphatically stated in his chirpy English accent, – you love this song! It's the fourth track on *Lust for Life* by our dear friend, Iggy Pop! Also, it's one of the best, or maybe only, songs ever written about riding the S-Bahn in Berlin. Remember when we went there? You loved it so much. Krishna gently encouraged me to remember one of the first vacations we took together, but I was unable to recall anything about it.

Abruptly, the channel changed again; all I was able to see was the ancient gray-and-white static from a black-and-white television set. I could faintly make out my own voice over the hum and hiss of the static.

- How long have I been like this? I meekly repeated this question over and over until my voice was but a whisper.

- Three months. Krishna answered my query simply and honestly.

I strained to ask the question again. Six months was the answer. Finally, with no reserves left, a ghost haunting my own body, I simply looked at him and nodded my head in lieu of speaking. The room spun as I strained to hear his reply.

AFTER AN INTERMINABLE WAIT FOR MORNING, doors began to quickly open and slam; I heard the distinct sound of the mentally ill shuffling down the hallway, no destination in mind, just wandering aimlessly in green slipper socks. Each day bled into the next without any distinction or differentiation – complete and utter time-lessness.

My body throbbed and ached as I slowly got out of bed; as I closed the door to my room, I was startled by the sound of rain pelting down on the window – SPLAT, SPLAT. The wind screamed like a banshee from an ancient Gaelic tale as I made my way to the bathroom. I disrobed and let my scrubs fall to the floor; they were stiff with perspiration. I turned on the shower and shuddered as I waited for the water to heat up.

Finally, I stepped into the scalding water, hoping it would sanitize me. I let the intense pressure from the faucet pound my neck and shoulders. I couldn't stand the smell of the anti-bacterial soap I was given, so I used shampoo to wash my body; my back was in constant pain as I bent over, with barely enough room to wash my feet. I washed what was left of my hair and turned off the water.

I stepped out of the shower into a steam-filled bathroom, the air heavy and wet with humidity. As I brushed my teeth, I was grateful that the condensation saved me from confronting my reflection in the mirror.

TEN

- Is your injection site still sore? Dr. Mueller questioned Connie.

She recoiled from him and leaned on the wall outside of her room; she started to pick at the freshly scabbed-over wound on her forearm, bursting with fresh blood and pus and then changed her mind. She covered her left arm and its gaping lesion with a childlike air of protection.

I ambled down the hallway towards the dining room, hoping that the intense pains in my stomach would be settled by a bit of food. My path was suddenly blocked by a nurse in the hallway; she was standing outside of a room with its door closed. Upon closer inspection, I noticed that this door had a large window that looked like a cage and a lock on the outside. A terrible stench seeped out from the small amount of space between the door and floorboards.

- Come on, Miss Lily. A petite nurse with dark hair and glasses pleaded with her patient to open the door.

- You have to open the door or go take a shower right now! You have to bathe. She pounded on the door this time; the only response she received was the sound of her patient creeping and pacing around in her room.

- NOW, MISS LILY, DON'T MAKE ME HELP YOU LIKE LAST TIME! The nurse's patience had run out, but her threats went unnoticed. Finally, she took out a set of keys from her pocket, braced herself, and forcefully unlocked the door to Miss Lily's room.

I continued walking towards the dining room, but as I passed the nurses' station, I heard a harsh female voice calling my name.

- Deborah.

- DEBORAH, COME HERE.

It took an immense effort to turn around, but I soon found myself lumbering back to the front desk.

- You've missed breakfast, I was briskly informed. – It's time for your meds – wait here.

I stood silently waiting for the incredibly grouchy nurse to complete the seemingly endless sequence of steps necessary to procure medicine; my eyes wandered to a miniature white paper cup already on the counter. It was filled with a cornucopia of pills: two enormous white pills, a small round blue pill, three miniature peach pills, and a giant of a dark blue and white pill that seemed to almost burst out of the confines of the minuscule paper cup.

- Those are for Lauren – not for you.

The nurse's stern reprimand sent a jolt through my entire body. My face flushed instantly with embarrassment, and I felt as if I had done something wrong, though I was unclear as to what this misdeed exactly was.

- This is your pill. Dr. Mueller increased your Cymbalta to 40mg.

She thrust two flimsy paper cups towards me with an air of expectancy. As I swallowed my pill, I felt her gaze on my throat.

I SLOWLY WALKED BACK to my room, intent on brushing my teeth and taking another scalding hot shower to ward off the evils I constantly felt encircling me. As I approached my room, I almost lost my balance as Alex crossed my path; he was pacing up and down the halls with intense speed and fervor, his focal point intent on something, or someone, far away.

As soon as I walked into my room, Dr. Mueller walked towards me with a palpable air of authority. He was holding a stack of yellow papers in his right hand. I looked at him in shock and confusion, and I felt his unkind brown eyes burrow into me.

- Deborah Hartung, we are officially extending your hold. I have your official commitment papers here. You are now on a 5152, which means we can hold you here for up to thirty days. At this point, you will be re-evaluated, and we will have the option to extend your hold for up to three months. If you are here for three months, we have the right to hold you indefinitely or transfer you to a state-run care facility.

- I...I don't understand. I looked at Dr. Mueller with utter confusion; he thrust the stack of papers at me in response.

I burst into tears and started to plead with him, - Let me out of here, please!

- Deborah, most people in your position show guilt or remorse for their actions; they are not so focused on leaving.

I looked up at him through bleary eyes and felt bewilderment penetrate and spread through the haze of my mind. I had no recollection of my recent actions, let alone something that would incite such tremendous amounts of guilt.

- Let me ask you a question: are you at all happy to be alive?

I began to cry hysterically, and the papers I held dropped to the floor and began to scatter across my room as a gust of cold air entered through the open door. Dr. Mueller silently observed me, and then, finally, he spoke:

- I think that's enough for today. With that, he walked out of my room.

ELEVEN

I sat hunched over on my bed, reeling from my interaction with Dr. Mueller. Occasionally, I lifted my pounding head up from my hands and stared at the rain pouring down outside the grime-covered window. My mind spun as I tried to make sense of my horrific circumstances and what actions led up to being held against my will in such a dire place. I tried in vain to remember what had happened, but treading through the muck and mire of my fractured mind was a treacherous affair – like crossing a haunted, misty moor at midnight – there was a hovering sense of danger with every step. Hours passed as I sat in the same folded-up position, dipping in and out of the murky depths of my memory, which only seemed to add to my confusion. Eventually, my limbs grew stiff and tired, and my stomach began to rumble, yet I refused to move a muscle and continued my vigilance, desperately trying to force my memory to work.

A strange shuffling sound startled me, and the next thing I knew, Connie was standing in my doorway.

- You have a ph-ph- phone call! She proclaimed this in an incredibly high pitched, childlike voice, complete with stutter. She had a big, goofy grin on her face; she clapped her hands suddenly and repeated herself.

- You have a ph-phone call! She jumped up and down and clapped with excitement, like a child trying to rouse her parents on Christmas morning so that she could open presents. As I finally looked up and acknowledged her, she immediately turned on her heels and ran away.

I tried in vain to move quickly, but my entire body was aching and sore; it took the last reserves of my strength and willpower to move from my bed and stand up. My feet tingled and I felt a numbing sensation shoot through my arms and hands; the tips of my fingers felt strange and dull.

When I finally made it out of my room and into the hallway, I was instantly overwhelmed by the harsh noises of the ward, the intense glow of the overhead lights and the smell of stale, recycled air that possessed an arctic chill. I could see Alex doing laps from my peripheral vision as I searched for the telephone with a confused look on my face.

Finally, amidst talking on the phone with a headset, shuffling through a stack of papers, and feverishly writing notes, a multitasking nurse took pity on me and mouthed to me, "I'll transfer your call." She pointed to her right; it took immense effort for my eyes to focus and track her short and chubby finger, but I eventually noticed an ancient, olive-green rotary phone attached to a stark white wall. The phone rang and rang; its shrill, high-pitched noise seemed to fill the ward and added to my complete and utter consternation.

- Hello? I whispered, terrified to find out who was on the other end of the phone.

- Debbie, honey. Hi. How are you?

I burst into tears in response to the question, for the voice was filled with kindness and it seemed to pierce through my fogginess. A woman's face flashed through my mind's eye – a pale face filled with freckles, with caring brown eyes and framed by a sea of fiery red, curly hair. Instinctively, I knew this woman to be an ally and a friend, yet I could not remember her name.

- It's Susan, honey.

I silently nodded as I tried in vain to force myself to remember this valuable information.

- Did the nurse give you the sweatshirt I left for you last night? She gingerly questioned. Again, I nodded 'yes,' forgetting that Susan could not see me.

- Thank you... The barely audible words trembled out of my mouth.

- Where am I? I pleaded.

- You're in the Outer Mission.

- What is this place? I desperately asked. I yearned to know where I was – and why.

- You're in the hospital, honey.

- But what kind of place is this? I questioned her with all the energy I possessed.

There was a long pause, and Susan audibly sighed.

- Well, my dear, to be perfectly honest, you're on the mental health ward.

Waves of terror and paranoia swept over me, and my legs felt wobbly and unstable. I braced myself against the cold concrete wall to avoid falling. Somehow, I managed to hold onto the phone with my free hand.

- Are you still there, honey? Susan questioned.

My breathing was rapid, and my chest felt like it might explode; my heart thudded and thumped into my ears as I struggled for breath. I was instantly drenched in sweat. Afraid of losing this lifeline, I forced myself to answer.

- Umm...yes.... I managed to get two words out between gasps for air.

- Mario's here at the shop with me. We're finishing up a

pair of custom shoes, and he really wants to say 'hello' to you. Hold on just a sec, and I will put him on the line –

I did not have the energy to protest, and before I knew it, I heard:

- Ciao, Bella. It was the thick accent of an Italian octogenarian. Mario sounded very far away, and I could barely understand what he was saying. It sounded like he said the word 'chocolate' again and again, but I could not be sure, for his voice was muffled and low.

Suddenly, the ringing in my ears paused, and I felt as if I had briefly dropped back into my body. It took all my willpower and energy to focus on what he was saying, but for a brief instant, Mario, Susan's business partner and staunch Catholic, was crystal clear:

– ...God will forgive you, but you have to pray the rosary. That is the correct way to pray -

That was the last thing I heard as I flopped down into the filthy, white plastic chair next to the wall. I sat there stupefied and let the phone drop out of my tight grip; I did not hear it hit the ground. I was more confused than ever before. Once again, there was an implication that I had done something so awful it needed forgiveness from God himself, yet I could barely remember my own name, let alone the sin I had committed. My eyes welled up and over-flowed with tears, and I felt as if someone had trampled on my heart with heavy combat boots.

TWELVE

As I came to, I slowly began to realize where I was: in the middle of the hallway, crumpled up on a child's size plastic chair; to add to this, I was entangled with a seemingly endless amount of green phone cord. Suddenly, I heard the all too familiar sound of a trolley being wheeled down the slippery hospital floor, followed by Connie's excitement.

- It's snack time! She exclaimed as she ran behind the cart and clapped her hands in anticipation of this momentous event.

- THEY HAVE CHOCOLATE CAKE! Connie screamed as her squeaky voice echoed throughout the hallway. She began to jump up and down, and her clapping increased to a fervor; the next thing I knew, she ran past me and once again proclaimed, - THEY HAVE CHOCO-LATE CAKE!

Connie's announcement of chocolate cake was a siren song that no mental patient could resist; a slow rustling sound began to fill the ward. Gaunt, ghostlike figures appeared seemingly out of nowhere with mouths hung open in anticipation of a sugary treat. Drool and dried, caked bits of spittle formed around their mouths as the line of drugged patients, all wearing the same purple scrubs, shuffled and followed the creaky trolley to the dining room.

- IS THERE someone here I can talk to? I asked as tears of confusion and guilt ran down my hollow cheeks. The same nurse who connected my phone call looked at me with exasperation; a flame of anger briefly flashed in her brown eyes.

- Like a pastor or a priest? Father Mick works in the main hospital, but you are not allowed to leave this unit until your doctor signs you out. She averted her eyes from mine and looked down at a stack of papers.

- No, I mean, a therapist...before I could finish my sentence, she interrupted me:

- We don't have those here. Who's your doctor? She waved her hand in annoyance – Never mind. I have your file right here. Dr. Mueller doesn't have time today.

The thought of having another interaction with Dr. Mueller filled me with dread; I turned around and walked away.

- Deborah. DEBORAH! I slowly turned around and saw a nurse with long grey hair and a kind face full of wrinkles. She leaned heavily on a cane. – I'll talk to you. Her pale green eyes were full of compassion, and they crinkled as she smiled. I was instantly assured that this was someone I could trust. – I will meet you in your room in ten minutes. She nodded her head and turned away, loping toward the medication closet.

PART 2

THE ETERNAL

Procession moves on, the shouting is over
Praise to the glory of loved ones now gone
Talking aloud as they sit round their tables
Scattering flowers washed down by the rain

Stood by the gate at the foot of the garden
Watching them pass like clouds in the sky
Try to cry out in the heat of the moment
Possessed by a fury that burns from inside
Cry like a child, though these years make me
    older

JOY DIVISION

THIRTEEN

I heard her cane – thump- and her supportive shoes hitting the floor in an even rhythm as she headed toward my room. Connie was rustling around in the room next to mine, talking to herself in her signature high-pitched tone; I could not make out what she was saying as the rain pelted down loudly against the windows, which were now clouded over with condensation. I sat on my bed and gripped my hands together to stop them from shaking; my feet were nestled into their slipper socks and touched the floor, but I could barely feel them as the sense of numbness and tingling seemed to increase exponentially each minute.

The nurse arrived at my door, heaving and out of breath; she leaned on the doorframe for a minute before she entered my room and placed herself on the bed opposite mine. I did not notice a nametag and did not think to ask her name, but she was instantly deemed "Kind Nurse" when I saw her look at me and smile gently.

- How do I get out? How do I get out? I was stuttering again and could not seem to get the complete sentence out of my mouth, but Kind Nurse instantly guessed my question.

- How do you get out of here? She leaned on her cane with both arms and sighed; her right leg was sticking straight out as it refused to bend.

I nodded in response to her question and anxiously awaited her reply.

She breathed in and out and shivered from the intense cold of the room. – I haven't had time to look at your file, so I don't know what happened before you got here, but the easiest way to get out is to take your meds, stop isolating and join the group activities. The doctors look for patients who are committed to getting better, and the first step after taking your medication is to interact with others and show up for your O.T. sessions. You will also want to have an aftercare plan of some sort; if I were you, I would agree to go to outpatient treatment as soon as it's suggested. *You have to play by their rules.*

I tried to process her suggestions; I could feel my mind trying to focus, but it was fuzzy again. By the time I was cognizant enough to thank Kind Nurse and ask her a few questions, I looked over to an empty bed across the room. I searched the hallway for her and walked by the nurses' station, hoping to get a glimpse of her, but she had vanished into thin air. Goosebumps covered my body as I wondered if she was just a hallucination or a figment of my imagination.

THE MOLDY, putrid smell of the Day Room engulfed me as I forced myself to participate in the task at hand: filling out a worksheet entitled, "Who Am I?" The sound of tiny golf pencils screeching on cheap paper filled the musty room; even Alex stopped his compulsive pacing to participate. Lauren sat next to me and shook and mumbled to herself while trying to grip her pencil. A new face stared at me from across the table; Aaron had emerged from his room for this occasion and sat in front of a blank worksheet. His attention was focused on me, and his red eyes and incredibly dilated pupils bore into me. I averted his stare and put all my energy into looking at the piece of paper in front of me.

I fiercely gripped my pencil to quell my shaking hand and wrote my name on the top of the paper as if I were a child in grade school. Finally, I was able to bring my mind into focus for a brief instant and answered the first question.

1. Write 3 positive words that describe yourself.

Creative, upbeat & smart

I stared at the next batch of questions for at least ten minutes and finally scribbled an answer to number four.

2. What single factor contributes to your self-esteem?
3. What do you consider to be your greatest accomplishment?
4. What would your best friend say is your most positive attribute?

Good listener

5. What was the most positive message that someone involved in your upbringing/guidance gave you (parents, grandparents, guardians, etc)?

I started to sweat profusely and felt immense pressure and

stress building behind my eyes as I tried to complete this simple exercise. It took all my energy to scribble down an answer to the final question.

6. What would you most like to be remembered for in your life?

Art and creativity

- Since we're a small group today, let's go around the table and share our answers. A deep female voice suggested this terrifying proposition. I looked up, and for the first time, I seemed to notice Tracy, our Occupational Therapist, seated at the head of the table. Her hair was dyed midnight blue and cropped short; she had a very stocky build and wore long sleeves to cover her arm tattoos. Even in the dappled light of the Day Room, I could see her mustache.

- Deborah, let's start with you.
Intense fear and dread filled the pit of my stomach. I looked at Tracy pleadingly, but all I received in return was a harsh stare.

- Deborah, you're new here, aren't you? I ignored her question and wished that I could disappear.

- Tell us a little about yourself, Deborah. I silently sat at the table, dumbstruck and full of utter confusion.

- DEBORAH, you're with us, right? Tracy was getting frustrated with me and could not help but raise her manly voice. I nodded my head in an attempt to answer her question.

Tracy repeated her question, this time with a slightly softer tone.

- Deborah, why are you here?
I looked up to find Tracy staring at me, imploring me

with her dark eyes to answer her question. I could not help but notice that Aaron, Alex, and Lauren seemed to mirror the immense discomfort that I felt. Once again, Tracy repeated her question.

- Deborah, why are you here?

I sat frozen in place; Tracy's question resounded again and again in my mind. *Deborah, why are you here?* My heart thumped uncontrollably, and I felt hot and claustrophobic. *Deborah, why are you here?* Suddenly, there was a bright and blinding flash of light in my eyes and my psyche was flooded with fragments of memories.

A man's strange voice questioned me: *It's time now. Have you changed your will?* The realization that the voice belonged to Bodhi, Aurelia's friend and my former spiritual teacher. *Make sure all the documents are signed.*

In my mind's eye, I saw myself in a state of complete and utter desperation. A plea for help. Silence. Anguish washed over me, yet the sane part of my consciousness guided me to make one final cry for help. I saw myself grab my phone and randomly hit the call button; I trembled as I waited for the sound of another human being. Finally, Aurelia's voice and then instantly, the loud, pulsating sound of a dial tone.

I let a blood-curdling, guttural scream escape, and it reverberated against the walls and surrounded me; I felt smothered. I clawed for the large bottle of vodka on my kitchen counter and the open vials of pills. In one gulp, I finished the pure grain alcohol and swallowed mounds of small, astringent pills. Glass broke above me, and I felt sharp shards rain down on me, followed by a haunting silence and then complete and utter darkness.

- Deborah, why are you here? Tracy's voice rattled me to the core, and I was instantly brought back to the present moment.

- Deborah, why are you here?

- I, I think I tried to kill myself. I whispered this, and as the words flew out of my mouth, I sat there in disbelief, and yet, on a deep level, I knew this was the horrible truth.

After a long and intense silence, I looked up at Tracy, Alex, Lauren, and Aaron with acute vulnerability and feeling almost dirty with shame; there were no kind eyes returning my stare. Instead, the entire group sat with their chins on their necks and eyes downcast on the table, for in this human factory of maladies, we became worse and more disoriented by the hour. We spiraled together, deeper and deeper, into a pool of delirium and disdain.

FOURTEEN

- GET ME MY ADDERALL, BITCH! SHE WAS A GODDAMN SERVICE DOG! WHAT HAVE YOU DONE WITH HER? DID YOU TAKE HER TO THE SPCA? I WANT MY ADDERALL NOW, YOU FUCKING BITCH!

A frightened woman's voice yelled out in response, - RESTRAINTS! TIFFANY, CALM DOWN – NOW!

There was a lot of running back and forth down the hallway, which reverberated across the entire ward. More profanities and demands spewed forth from the mouth of the new patient; then she screamed loudly, and finally, there was silence.

My heart was palpitating, and I felt truly afraid; I quivered in my bed. Although a part of me was terrified of the new patient and her dramatic arrival, I tried to will myself to sleep, as I could feel exhaustion creeping up and over me. I let my heavy eyelids close, and for the first time in days, I felt myself drifting off into a deep sleep. Suddenly, the door to my room was thrust open, and bright light once again set my retinas ablaze with pain.

- Deborah, you have a new roommate, a male voice informed me before stomping away. He left the door wide open in his wake, and the fluorescent light continued to flood into the room.

A thin figure with neon green hair and two inches of blonde roots showing tentatively walked into the room. I was instantly wide awake and on guard as her anger was palpable, and I could feel it across the room. *Was this the infamous Tiffany who had just arrived?* I was instantly petrified that she was my new roommate. I stared at the new arrival across from me, and I could sense that despite her animosity, she was also scared on the inside, standing there in her standard-issue purple scrubs, which were two sizes too big for her small frame. My new roommate clenched a brown paper bag, and when I read *Jamie* written in large letters on the outside, I let out a huge sigh of relief just as she flopped down on her bed. She looked so vulnerable to me, and I couldn't help but notice that she was shivering.

- They'll give you extra blankets — just ask one of the nurses, I gently offered.

Jamie rolled over onto her side and pulled the thin sheet and blanket over her head in response.

I jumped out of bed to close the door, only to find myself hesitating. *What if she murders me in my sleep?* I looked over at Jamie sleeping and reassured myself that she was harmless; I gently closed the door and crawled back into bed — leaving the lights on just in case.

THE DINING ROOM was packed with new faces the next morning; I was trying to take in all the fresh additions to the unit, but my thoughts were interrupted by a female voice loudly shouting.

- ARE YOU GOING TO DRINK THAT JUICE? CAN I GET MORE JUICE? I looked down at the orange juice in a tiny plastic container on my tray and wondered if she was yelling at me.

- I SAID I WANT MORE JUICE! ARE YOU LISTENING TO ME?

I carefully sneaked a look at the new patient: she seemed to be my age, in her late thirties, barely five feet tall, and had dyed green hair, which was fading and now looked yellow. At least five inches of light brown roots showed. Her red rayon jacket covered her purple top, which she had rolled up to expose her taut stomach. She also had an orange wristband which read, *High Alert Patient*. For a second, I wondered if she was my roommate; fear gripped me, and I pushed my food away. I covertly looked at her face and saw that she had big pimples filled with white puss all over her face, a mouth full of rotting teeth, and the look of pure crazy in her dark green eyes; I knew this to be the look of someone who was addicted to speed or maybe crystal meth and living on the edge, if not homeless. Danger emanated from her, and I turned away as she began to shovel her breakfast down her mouth, screaming once again about juice between mouthfuls. I felt satisfied that she was not Jamie, as she looked nothing like her, and after a sharp pain in my forehead and a lot of thinking on my part, I realized that she had to be Tiffany.

I tried to eat my breakfast, but I felt queasy and had no appetite. I looked around the room and noticed that there was an older man wearing fetid, dirty street clothes sitting at the end of the table. I wondered why some patients were allowed articles of their own clothing, while I was forced to wear the same sweat-drenched scrubs day after day.

Roger was written on the man's bracelet, and as the smell of his clothes wafted toward me, I felt sick to my stomach. He had no teeth, and his mouth was quite gummy, yet this did not stop him from inhaling his applesauce, yogurt, and scrambled eggs.

I rushed back to my room, desperate to brush my teeth and to take a shower. Jamie's bed was empty and unmade; she was nowhere in sight.

I turned the shower on and vigorously brushed my teeth as the water heated up. Just as I took off my dirty scrubs, I heard the door to my room forcefully open. I panicked as I heard a familiar female voice yell – WHO'S IN THE BATHROOM? JAMIE OR DEBORAH?

I cracked open the bathroom door and poked my head out, instantly recognizing Tracy, the Occupational Therapist. I wondered why she was doing a safety check, as that duty was usually done by nurses.

- It's me, Debbie. She did not seem to recognize me at all.

- What's going on in there? She demanded.

- I'm just about to take a shower. I tried to reassure her by repeating my statement, but it clearly was not working. Tracy walked towards me, getting closer to the bathroom door each second. I began to panic.

- Don't come in! I yelped. I quickly tried to grab a towel to cover myself, as I knew there was not a lock on the bathroom door. My plea raised all of Tracy's suspicions, and the next thing I knew, she used all her strength to thrust the bathroom door open, convinced she was going to find a troubling situation at hand.

Unfortunately, all she saw was me fumbling for a towel that was draped over the shower. In a moment of fright, I dropped it and turned to face her, forgetting that I was completely naked. Tracy was instantly shocked and embarrassed, and the next thing I knew, she bolted from my room with her eyes glued to the floor, all the while mumbling to herself. I couldn't help but be amused at the absurdity of the situation, and I let out a tiny giggle as I saw her large figure running out of my room.

FIFTEEN

- Let's warm up! Part of healing is improving your physical health. A huge grin emanated from a young female face, and she began to march in place. There was something about this twenty-something that was familiar to me, but I just could not place her.

- That's it! Just start moving! I know it will feel good! The very enthusiastic woman increased her speed and raised her knees up and down in perfect harmony; she seemed to have an internal metronome that guided her every movement.

- Oh, by the way, I'm Jen, your Occupational Therapist for this morning. Silly me, I forgot to mention this. She smiled at her own error and encouraged us, a group of heavily medicated mental patients standing in a circle, all dressed in purple scrubs with glazed eyes, to keep up with her pace. Legs began to wobble in place; knees seemed to magically lift off the ground, and limbs moved of their own accord. No one in the small group was able to keep up with Jen, yet everyone enjoyed it as the circle was now filled with the sound of panting and goofy, toothy grins on many faces. The floor of the Day Room began to shake underneath us, and we were given our next task: to act out our favorite sport while the rest of the group emulated our movements.

- Deborah, why don't you go first?

Jen encouraged me while I stood frozen in place, annoyed that I was called on first, once again. Also, I was quite sure I knew Jen and my mind tried to figure out where I had met her while simultaneously sifting through a life of failed sporting activities. I must have been on autopilot because the next thing I knew, I felt my body slowly moving into a yoga pose. I swayed back and forth and tried to lift one knee on top of the other while bending at my waist, sticking my bum slightly out, and moving my hands into prayer position while very carefully straightening my back. I held the pose for about five seconds before toppling over.

- Nice! Tree pose! Does anyone else here like yoga? Jen looked around the room, only to be met with a group of very confused faces, unsure of which of my very ungraceful movements to copy.

- Let's move on! Lauren, why don't you show us your favorite sport?

Lauren looked terrified, and I saw limbs shaking. After what felt like ten minutes, she stepped forward with her right knee, then she hesitated a bit, but finally began to swing her right arm across her body and almost over her shoulder.

- Tennis! Good work, Lauren. Is everyone having fun?

Jen continued to march as the group mulled over her question; she was starting to remind me of an aerobics instructor from the late 1980s and I was taken aback at her use of the word 'fun,' as being held against my will in a psych ward was not exactly my idea of a good time. No one else seemed bothered by her choice of adjectives, and her question was met with bobbing heads, and smiling, marching mental patients.

- I've got one! A tall and very thin man in his late forties called out to the group in a thick New York accent.

- William, that's great! Go ahead and show us! Jen was getting very excited – she had an active participant and even better than that, a volunteer.

William stepped slightly forward with his right foot and bent his right knee while his hands grasped and swung an invisible bat.

- Baseball! That's great, William. I know you're new here, why don't you introduce yourself to the group?

William stopped marching and hung his head down for a moment. Slowly, he raised it; I could barely see his face because it was covered with a brown, scraggly, bushy beard, but I could make out a bright, bulbous red nose typical of alcoholics. He also had sad-looking dark green eyes with deep crow's feet lines.

- I'm Will. As he looked around the room, I could feel Will's penetrating stare.

- Like I said, I'm Will, and I'm... his voice trailed off, but I had the feeling that he had a lot more to share.

- Ok, that's enough cardio for today. Let's move to the table and begin our next project.

A sense of relief was felt by the entire group after Jen's announcement; heads around the circle nodded in approval and exhausted bodies instantly stopped marching and began to slowly meander to the wobbly table in the corner of the Day Room.

I DUTIFULLY GRIPPED my mini pencil and tried my best to fill out the form in front of me, although I doubted it would really do me any good.

Fourteen Questions to Help You Remember What Makes You Feel Better:

1. My favorite movie of all time is...*Harold and Maude*
2. My favorite song of all time is...*Lady Stardust (David Bowie)*
3. My greatest accomplishment is...*Starting my own business with Krishna*
4. My perfect day...*Drinking chai with Krishna, listening to music, making art & going out to dinner.*
5. My most cherished possession is...*Mix tapes (from Krishna)*
6. My favorite cheer-me-up music is...*electronica (LCD Soundsystem)*
7. I enjoy reading...*Irvine Welsh*
8. My fantasy vacation...*Tulum, Mexico*
9. I don't do it much, but I enjoy...*cooking*
10. If I could lighten up a little, I'd let myself...*enjoy life*
11. If I weren't so stingy with myself, I'd buy myself... *a weekend away*
12. Two people I admire are...*Krishna & David Bowie*
13. I am proud of myself for...?
14. I'm grateful for...*my friends & family*

- Ok, good work everyone! Let's go around the table now; please share your answers to question number three. I would love to hear about your accomplishments.

Jen's eternal optimism began to irritate me, but I reminded myself that participating in group activities was contributing to my eventual freedom.

I was relieved when Jen called on Lauren first; she grasped her paper with her wobbly hands and held it close to her face as she squinted to read her handwriting. After a few minutes of scrutinizing the paper, she apologized. –

Sorry, everyone...I just can't see that well at the moment. My meds do that to me sometimes.

- It's ok, Lauren. Why don't you just put the paper down and tell us about your greatest achievement? Jen was encouraging, but I had the sense that this was an order, not a request.

Apparently, Lauren felt the same because she began to shake heavily and dropped her paper on the table. She took a few deep breaths and then quietly spoke.

- I'm most proud of getting into graduate school.

- Where were you studying, Lauren? Jen asked. I doubted the relevance of sharing personal information with this group, but I could tell Lauren felt pressured to continue.

- Ahhh...I'm going to UCSF. Lauren looked down for a moment and then back up at the group. – I'm in their nursing school program; I want to be a psychiatric nurse.

Lauren's voice began to fade into the distance, and suddenly, I could almost feel the neurotransmitters in my brain firing as my mind struggled to come back to life; something she said triggered this unusual experience.

My heart began to race, and then suddenly, the fog in my mind lifted, and I was instantaneously able to remember details from my past: I also studied in San Francisco for my undergrad degree. I was a passionate student of neuropsychology. More information flooded my brain, and I recalled receiving a letter from the University Of San Francisco on thick, embossed letterhead paper, in which the dean of the university congratulated me on my grades and dedication to psychology; it ended with the school extending an offer to pay for my continued studies in either their masters or Ph.D. programs.

Less than a year after receiving this letter, which gave me an immense self-esteem boost and felt like a reward for my disciplined learning, I had a massive nervous break-down. The impetus for the breakdown escaped me, and while the minutiae of the event were fuzzy, I remembered that it happened during my junior year, and it was so terrible that I was forced to drop out of school for a semester. When I returned to the university, I was a shell of my former self. It took every fiber of my being to get out of bed and attend classes; the zeal I had for learning vanished, and I felt lethargic and broken in body and mind. Additionally, the mental acuity I had twelve months prior had utterly and completely disappeared, as had the offer of a scholarship. I was ashamed of my brain fog and the obvious signs of depression I exuded, and my advisor, Dr. Hansen, felt similarly: her brightest student and protégé was gone, and this caused her immense frustration, for I was supposed to be her after hours tutor and the president of an academic society that she headed. The embarrass-ment intensified, and I knew that I did not possess the acumen to complete my final neuropsychology research project or the accompanying classes. In desperation, I quickly switched to visual art as my major, as I had always loved to paint, and I knew this to be one of the easiest majors at school; even through this struggle, I was deter-mined to get my degree.

Instantly, confusion settled upon me once again, and I found myself somewhat befuddled, sitting around a dirty table in a dingy room with my fellow psych ward patients.

Jen next focused her attention on Alex, who suddenly appeared at the table. He was compulsively pacing the halls during the exercise portion of our occupational therapy session but wandered into the Day Room when Jen some-what forcefully asked him to join the group.

Alex flatly refused to share his greatest accomplishment in life and began to compulsively stroke his chin when suddenly he blurted out, - The Lion King is my favorite movie, though.

Jen seemed satisfied with this answer and moved on to question Aaron.

- Aaron, would you like to tell us a little about your achievement? Aaron continued to stare straight ahead, his focal point on the bookcase in the corner. His eyes were bloodshot and puffy; his enormous, glassy pupils were completely still. Finally, he blinked and continued to sit silently in his chair.

Jen gently prodded him, - Aaron, is there anything you would like to share with us? I was unsure if he even heard the question as he was clearly in an over-medicated state and possibly psychotic.

- I, um, like sushi. Aaron finally spoke, and clearly, it was hard work for him. Jen insisted on trying to coerce more information out of him.

- What's your favorite sushi restaurant?

- We. Be. Su. Shi. on Val. En. Cia. Stree.t. I was surprised that he liked sushi so much and once I pieced together that he was talking about We Be Sushi in the Mission, I realized that I knew the exact location of the small restaurant. I was elated that I could picture this small hole-in-the-wall so clearly in my mind's eye and blurted out, - I know exactly where that is!

Aaron slowly swiveled his head to face me, and I felt his gaze wash over me and eventually focus on the wall behind my head. There was something creepy about him, and I instantly regretted saying anything at all. He did not acknowledge my comment, and Jen quickly put her focus on me once again.

- Deborah, you're up next. Please share your accomplishments with the group.

I looked down at my paper and tried to find the words to

describe my answer to Jen's question, but my tongue was instantly tied, and I felt her peering gaze, which made me incredibly nervous. I tried in vain to recall details of the small business Krishna and I ran together, but they eluded me. I could not remember the name of our business, only vague details, and the feeling of being very proud of it and a bit protective of this memory.

- Umm...my partner and I had a small business... running it made me feel very proud.

I looked up at the group, but the only eyes that returned my gaze belonged to Lauren and, of course, Jen.

- Tell us more about your business; this is fascinating! As soon as Jen made this proclamation, I clammed up and once again, felt my cheeks flush as if I was a shy schoolgirl called upon during class.

- Ah, it was a baby clothing company. I think we used organic cotton... I slowly shared the only things that I knew for sure, but I felt clumsy in my explanation, and by the time I conjured up a few more distant memories, the moment had passed, and no one seemed to want to hear them anyway.

- Let's move on to you, William. Tell us about your accomplishment.

William seemed very shaky and terrified when Jen put him on the spot, but he slowly regained his composure.

- I'm....I'm William, and the best thing I ever did was sponsor Little Liam, a kid I took care of in New York. Instantly, his mood darkened, and it was clear that an internal war of emotions, brain chemistry, alcohol detoxification, and disturbing memories was taking place. He blurted out, - I lost custody of Little Liam on account of my drinking. He shook his head and began to quietly sob.

Jen tried her best to console him from across the table,

but it was clear she was at a loss for words. – Is there anything else you would like to share, William?

- I'm the sick fuck who tried to jump off the Golden Gate Bridge last night.

William hung his head, and a part of him was clearly relieved to have shared this burden with the group, who, for the most part, had not noticed his sadness or registered his bombshell. I felt my heart break for William; I looked over to him and tried to convey my empathy, but his eyes were vacant, as the pain of his past had once again taken him from the present moment.

SIXTEEN

I walked out of the Day Room and made a beeline for my room; I was tired and needed to rest, so much so that I was willing to do so even if my roommate was present. As I dragged my aching limbs down the hallway, I was immediately cut off by a short, stout figure in blue scrubs. The nurse was running so quickly that his glasses flew off his head, and he had to stop to pick them up, fumbling around blindly on the dirty floor with his hands until they felt the plastic of the glasses frame. As soon as the thick frames were fastened around his ears, he was off again.

- IS HE ON HIS WAY NOW? He screamed to another nurse at the front desk. The loud static of a walkie-talky followed, and bits of a conversation I could not make out. I stood in place, trying my best not to be knocked over by the chaos that had just erupted.

- HE WAS JUST DISCHARGED FROM THE CARDIO UNIT. HE'S ALMOST HERE! The other nurse screamed this update down the hallway; her high-pitched voice reverberated throughout the ward.

The male nurse ran to the very end of the hallway and opened a series of doors that I had assumed were more rooms for patients. They, in fact, housed an enormous washing machine, a dryer, and extra scrubs. My mind started to feel more alive, and I realized that the entire time, I was forced to wear dirty scrubs so thick with sweat and grime they almost stood upright on their own while a clean pair was just waiting for me at the end of the hallway. I could feel the anger and frustration rise as my eyes widened, and I glimpsed the enormous stash of clean, purple scrubs. I yearned for fresh clothing, and my body was suddenly alight with energy, and my mind immediately awoke from its slumber: I planned to make a mad dash towards the magical closet of cleanliness.

I casually walked into the hallway and looked around to make sure I was not being observed; for once, there was no one around. It did not occur to me that the nurse I saw just seconds before might return; I could only think about the fact that only a few steps separated me from freshly laundered scrubs. Just as I was approaching the closet, I was almost knocked down by a man who was also running towards the closet, screaming at the top of his lungs.

- WHAT SIZE IS HE? 3X? The whirling blue dervish asked.

- AT LEAST A 4X! The quick reply was once again very loud, and her voice was like nails on a chalkboard to me.

The male nurse I saw just minutes before had returned; he ran from cupboard to cupboard, searching for the largest pair of scrubs on hand. I quickly removed myself from his path of frenetic energy and retreated to the Day Room, where I observed him shake his head and swear under his breath. He was beaten: the largest size on hand was 2X, and from what he was told, that was not enough fabric to decently cover half of his incoming patient.

- TYRONE! OVER HERE! The nurse shouted and

waved his hands, trying in vain to get his new patient's attention. As he turned, I could see his nametag: *Jack Harrison, Psychiatric Nurse*.

I knew it was rude to stare, but I was suddenly enthralled with the drama unfolding in front of my eyes, and sheer adrenaline coursed through my veins. Besides, I had not had any entertainment for days, and the television in the Day Room was continuously stuck on the weather channel. I stepped back from the hallway so that my feet were technically within the confines of the Day Room and tried to look inconspicuous, which was completely unnecessary, as I was the only soul in the room, and Nurse Jack was distracted and too busy to notice that I was watching him like a hawk.

I heard Tyrone before I saw him: the ground underneath my feet shook, and I heard heavy panting and breathing as he inched his way closer to me. Then I smelled him; he reeked of sweat and body odor, and he had a strange moldy smell oozing out of his pores, which wafted down the ward before his arrival. When he finally made his way halfway down the hallway, he was breathing so heavily I thought he might be having an asthma or heart attack. He looked completely befuddled as he made his way toward Nurse Jack, dragging his heels and dripping with perspiration. Tyrone was in his late thirties, with a bald head, and he stood around six feet, five inches tall. He must have weighed at least four hundred pounds; Tyrone was gargantuan in size and clad in an enormous hospital gown, which did not even begin to cover his massive girth. The dark flesh of his back was exposed, and his buttocks were bursting out of the shorts he was given as underwear; his skin was a dark ebony shade, and it was dry and cracked in the places that were not engulfed in sweat.

- You made it, man. Good work, Tyrone. Nurse Jack

was genuinely proud that Tyrone had made it down the hallway; he patted him on the shoulder while Tyrone stood in place, his chest heaving and gulping in air.

- This is the Day Room, where you will spend most of your time. We're still making up your room, so have a seat here, and I will be back in a few minutes. Nurse Jack gently turned Tyrone to face the Day Room, and when he lifted his heavy head up, he stared directly at me as I was still standing in the entranceway. He had large, vacant brown eyes with jaundiced sclera; his face was puffy, and his double chin was large and pronounced, and it seemed to be covered in dried drool. I wanted to be frightened of him, but I could tell that he was not fully cognizant and, therefore, seemed less of a threat than I originally imagined this giant of a man to be.

Nurse Jack gently led him into the room as I quickly stepped aside to avoid physical contact with either of them. Tyrone immediately plopped down on the threadbare sofa, which made a loud squeaking noise in response. I could hear springs popping one after another, like fireworks on the Fourth of July. I saw the base of the sofa strain and almost break as Tyrone shifted his weight and tried to get comfortable; it sounded like the poor couch was groaning underneath his enormity. Tyrone took up the entire couch and as soon as he turned his gaze to the television, he immediately began to blink and squint as if he was having trouble seeing the large screen.

- Do you need some glasses? Nurse Jack asked. Tyrone grunted, and Nurse Jack was again at his side and bending over backwards to help him while I stood there, feeling completely invisible.

- I will go into the lost and found closet and see if I can find you some glasses. Eventually, Tyrone made a strange snort and moved his head up and down in response, but it was too late, as Nurse Jack had already left the room with a bounce in his step.

- WHAT SIZE ARE YOU? A middle-aged woman with dark hair, olive skin, and tattooed eyeliner demanded.

- Um... I finally made it to the closet filled with pristine scrubs, folded neatly in rows and the only thing that separated me from complete and utter cleanliness was figuring out my size of scrubs.

- I think I'm a medium. The woman, whose nametag read 'Tonya' and who was wearing salmon pink scrubs, frowned and looked me over with her hazel eyes. I was not sure what this shade of pink scrubs meant on the psychiatric unit pecking order, but I assumed she was an orderly or maybe some kind of nurse's assistant. Her deep, penetrating stare was starting to make me uncomfortable.

- You're a small. Definitely a small. As Tonya made this proclamation, she was still fixated on my body, I don't think her eyes met mine once.

- Ok... I was in no mood to argue and was quite happy to take whatever scrubs I was given. My eyes glimpsed the rows of purple fabric in the closet again, and I held out my hands as if waiting to receive a precious gift.

Instead of reaching into the closet and handing me my scrubs, Tonya hesitated and started to stare at me again.

- Hmmm...medium, let's go with medium. Tonya said this mostly to herself as her gaze was now locked on my chest. – Maybe a small? She vacillated again and again while I stood there feeling completely undressed by her eyes.

Finally, I got up all the courage I had and tried my best to sound firm. – I'll take a medium. No 'please' or 'thank you', I just stated my preferred size. This seemed to get through to her and as I felt the rough cotton and polyester blend fabric placed in my hands, I instantly felt elated. I was heading straight back to my room to take a shower and then I would don my new outfit and feel clean from the inside out.

SEVENTEEN

- NICORETTE! I WANNA HAVE MY NICORETTE!
NICORETTE! I WANNA HAVE MY NICORETTE!

Connie demanded this again and again, and the cranky nurse I recognized from earlier in the week was not impressed; for the most part, she ignored Connie's persistent cries to quelch her nicotine cravings and continued to stare at her computer screen.

- Not yet, Connie, you still have two hours to go. The nurse repeated this at least two more times, with slight annoyance in her voice, while she continued typing.

- I NEED IT NOW! YOU HAVE TO GIVE IT TO ME! Connie loudly made this proclamation, and it seemed as if the entire psych ward went quiet afterwards. Minutes before, my new and immaculate scrubs had given me the courage to leave my room, but now I shivered and wished that I had not been lurking around the nurses' station again. I had a feeling that this showdown of wills was not going to end well.

The nurse stopped typing and looked up from her computer with utter disgust and contempt oozing from every pore. She scared me, and I imagined her to be some sort of wicked creature out of a Grimm's fairytale. Her nametag was hidden, but Cranky Nurse paused and took a deep breath in, and then she exhaled strong coffee breath with a faint scent of mildew. I scrunched up my nose and tried to prevent my gag reflex from kicking in; her withered hands came up from the desk, and she clasped them underneath her sagging chin and looked Connie directly in the eye.

- I don't have to do anything a patient tells me to do on this ward, Connie, especially not you. Let me remind you that I'm in charge here, NOT YOU! Cranky Nurse's words dripped with rancor and sent goosebumps down my arms; I watched Connie wince and lope away into the Day Room, head hung, lips downturned, and face locked into an intense frown. Seconds later, she was quickly walking back towards Cranky Nurse, yet she was almost smiling. It seemed as if Connie had no recollection of their previous interaction, which had occurred merely a minute earlier.

- Can I use the phone? Connie asked, in a polite tone and almost mischievous expression now on her face.

Cranky Nurse looked exhausted and sighed deeply, once again filling the room with her stale breath. I covered my mouth and nose with my hand as she silently gave a black cordless phone to Connie, who immediately dialed a number she knew by heart and began happily chatting in either Mandarin or Cantonese. Connie walked down the hallway with the phone glued to her ear, and I saw her curl up on her bed with it, like a baby holding a precious toy.

I HURRIEDLY RIFLED through the papers on my nightstand, constantly thinking to myself, *it has to be here somewhere*. Finally, underneath a mound of paperwork and occupational therapy projects, I gleaned the tiny scrap of paper with a messy and childlike version of my own handwriting on it. I scrutinized the page, and in tiny letters on the left-hand side of the page, I saw Dr. Gerrard's phone number. Connie's use of the mysterious black cordless phone gave me an idea, and it was my only chance of liberation from this psychiatric prison. I knew that Dr. Gerrard cared about me as a patient and furthermore, she was a good psychiatrist with a very exclusive practice in the Marina neighborhood of San Francisco. I had been a loyal patient for a decade and paid handsomely for her services, and now it was time to call in a favor.

Cranky Nurse had disappeared from the nurses' station and was replaced by the overly friendly and happy Jack Harrison; I could not believe my luck. I steadied myself and approached the counter; Nurse Jack looked up from his computer screen instantly and smiled at me.

- How are you doing, kid? Nurse Jack asked with actual care and concern in his voice. I was shocked at his kindness, so much so that I felt a bit choked up and momentarily forgot about my plan of action.

- Do you need something? He asked with incredible sincerity and instantly began to look through an enormous navy binder.

- According to this, it looks like you've taken all of your meds today. Oh, and no Xanax for you! He had a bit of an impish grin on his face when he said this, and I felt that there was an implication that I was missing.

- If you're having anxiety, I can only give something that's not in the Benzo family...

His voice trailed off, and I immediately felt distracted and bewildered. Judging from his reaction to me, I must have appeared incredibly nervous and on the verge of a panic attack; this was not how I wanted to project myself. I steadied my nerves and forced myself to continue with my mission.

- May I use the phone? I asked with the most sincerity and politeness I could muster. I noticed that my hands were shaking, so I clasped them together with all my strength, for fear of losing my precious piece of paper. I kept them underneath the high countertop, hidden from his sight.

- Oh! Ok. With that, he stretched out his right arm and reached for the black cordless phone Connie used. Nurse Jack pointed to the intake room across from the nurses' station and motioned for me to use it for my phone call; it was sparse, with a desk and computer facing a small bed. As I sat down on the bed, the disposable paper lining made a loud crackling and crinkling noise. I sat as still as possible and felt a flutter of hope as I turned on the phone with my unsteady right hand and gripped the torn piece of paper with Dr. Gerrard's number in my left hand as if it were my most prized possession. The phone rang and rang. I hung up and dialed the number again, this time vowing to leave a message once I heard her distinctive, low, gravelly voice.

You've reached the office of Dr. Jennifer Gerrard. My practice is currently full, and I am not accepting new patients. If you are an existing patient, you are welcome to leave a message, and I will respond as quickly as possible. If this is a medical emergency, please hang up and dial 911. Thank you. Beep!

Salty tears welled up in my eyes and started to trickle down my face; I was immediately choked up, but I forced myself to be strong and to leave a message, albeit tearful and pleading.

- Dr. Ger-rard, it's Debbie... Debbie Hartung. I'm stuck in this horrible place; please transfer me to a private hospital. I can pay, I promise! Please, please help me. Can you call or visit me? Please?

I was cut off by a shrill noise, and a robotic male voice informed me that my message was starting to exceed the limitations of Dr. Gerrard's voicemail; if I wanted to send it, I had to press the * key immediately. I summoned all the strength I had into my right index finger, and I pressed * with all my might as if my finger were a magical wand.

EIGHTEEN

Positive Focus

Picture these images to help you focus on a POSITIVE MENTAL ATTITUDE!

1. Picture a time or situation when you felt proud of yourself.

2. Picture one positive thing you do well.

3. Picture one of your roles or responsibilities in which you feel positive.

4. Picture one positive way you stay healthy or take care of your body.

5. Picture one positive characteristic you like best about yourself.

6. Picture one positive way you communicate or relate to others.

7. Picture one positive way you stay young at heart.

8. Picture one way you cope with stress.

9. Picture one way you can help yourself stay positive.

Each box pictured on the worksheet was approximately two inches by two inches and had room for an illustration. Without any hesitation, I grabbed a red marker from the middle of the table. Before the Occupational Therapist could even begin describing the activity, I began coloring the enormous camera that was illustrated in the upper left-hand side of the paper; *Positive Focus* was written sideways on the camera's lens, and the letters seemed to be begging to be filled in with a contrasting color. I helped myself to a yellow marker. I was in my own world, and the simple act of coloring comforted me; I slowly felt my body relax as I completely tuned out the female voice issuing directions to me and the rest of my fellow patients, seated once again around the table in the Day Room. The only noise that could penetrate my laser focus was the gentle pitter-patter of the rain falling on the thick glass doors that lined the back of the Day Room.

Ever the abiding student, I carefully wrote my name above the camera, and with great relief, I noticed that my hand was not shaking as much as it had been the last few days and that my handwriting looked semi-normal. The directions seemed self-explanatory, and I continued to draw inside the empty boxes. I was surprised that I was able to recall a time when I felt proud and drew a sloppy, childlike sketch of a successful art show Krishna, and I organized and participated in.

For the second box, I sketched a large piece of lined paper and a pen to illustrate something I did well. The third box seemed easy, and I drew a stick figure of myself walking Lucky, the aged miniature poodle I took for a daily walk. A large glass of water with H_2O written on it filled the fourth box, and it seemed like a simple way to take care of myself. I was in deep concentration and somewhat enjoying myself as I quickly drew an easel with a mountain on another piece of paper and wrote the word, *creative*, in the fifth empty box, symbolizing the characteristic I liked best about myself. A very large and round man's face, with a big, goofy grin, was the only way I could communicate the act of smiling, the positive way I could communicate and relate to others. A quick sketch of a tree, grass, and sun with radiating beams and the words, *Playing Outside*, filled the seventh box and represented a way for me to stay young at heart. The best way to cope with stress had always been a brisk walk up some of San Francisco's steepest hills and I tried to replicate this act in box eight. A smiling stick figure with open arms, poised for a hug, was the best way I could help myself stay positive.

I felt a sense of contentment starting to build inside of me as I looked at my drawings with a touch of pride; they were childlike and simple, but the very act of creating simultaneously filled me with an overwhelming sense of purpose and inner peace. Unfortunately, my bubble of serenity swiftly burst when I heard a chair being dragged across the hard, faux wood of the Day Room. The sound was shrill and piercing. I trembled and raised my eyes from my paper to see Tyrone placing the offensive chair next to me. As he plonked down, I could see the cheap wood shudder beneath his immense weight; the tremendously large hospital gown he was wearing split open and his flesh spilled out for all to see, and his body's distinct, fetid odor filled the room.

- Tyrone! It's so lovely of you to join us. A new Occupational Therapist, Mary, enthusiastically welcomed Tyrone to the group project of the day. In response, Tyrone simply grunted and nodded his head.

- Let's get you a worksheet...let me see here. Mary mumbled to herself while fumbling beneath a large navy-blue binder and stacks of paper. Finally, she retrieved the blank worksheet for Tyrone.

I kept my head down and stared at the drawings on the worksheet; I could feel Tyrone's eyes bore into me, and I was extremely cautious not to meet his intense gaze. Eventually, I heard lumbering footsteps. Out of the corner of my eye, I saw Mary, a stocky redhead with a face full of freckles, handing Tyrone a sheet of paper and a few markers. She quickly walked back to her place at the head of the table.

- Great! While Tyrone is finishing his worksheet, let's get started and share. Mary's excitement was met with silence from the group, and for the first time all morning, I looked up and noticed that Alex, Lauren, and William were all sitting around the table with their eyes intently focused on their worksheets, carefully avoiding Mary's gaze.

- Alex, let's start with you. Can you please show us your drawings and explain what a few of the illustrations mean? Let's start with the first three boxes.

I raised my head and saw Alex, who appeared to be very lucid, hold up his worksheet; each box was filled with exquisite pencil drawings scaled to proportion and complete with shading and extreme detail. I scanned the boxes and remained in awe; *how had he finished such beautiful drawings in under twenty minutes?*

- Ummm.... I felt proud of myself when I got into school for computers. Alex nervously scanned the room, and his right hand instantly began to compulsively touch his beard, but all eyes in the room were on his drawing of a computer inside 'box one' of his worksheet. It was the most perfect drawing of an original Apple computer from the 1980s that I had ever seen; Alex's ability to render something so realistic in a short amount of time astonished me, and I suddenly felt embarrassed by my own rudimentary drawings.

- Wow, that's a great drawing, Alex. I can tell that you must have been really proud to go to school for computers.

Alex nodded his head in response, but he was quite

careful not to divulge any additional information about himself.

- Can I ask where you went to school? Mary must have sensed that Alex was uncomfortable talking about this aspect of his life and pushed him to speak about it for what I assumed she thought was for his own good.

- Connecticut. New Haven, Connecticut. Alex was visibly uncomfortable after sharing this information. We sat in silence while Mary strategized whether to back down or go on the offensive again; we were all just pawns on her chess board, awaiting her next move. While Mary plotted her next move, Lauren caught my eye from across the table, which took me by surprise. She tried to raise her eyebrows but failed. It did not matter, though, as I seemed to know exactly what she was implying. I had the same thought: *Alex went to Yale to study computer science.*

Finally, Mary made her move. – What's in box number two? I was stupefied by her question, as Alex's second box was clearly filled with expertly drawn dental floss.

- It's dental floss, Alex answered in a calm tone. I'm not allowed to use it here, but before my hospitalizations, I took really good care of my teeth. I focused on Alex's choice of words: *hospitalizations*. Plural. I wondered how many hospital hallways he had paced in his time. I felt chills run up and down my arms as I suspected he had spent years on various psychiatric wards and was clearly not getting any better. A strange feeling that I was being watched interrupted my thoughts about Alex's hospitalization record, and I turned to find Tyrone staring at me and smiling a big, gap-toothed grin, and he began to grunt excitedly.

I made the mistake of making eye contact with Tyrone, and this caused him to become more animated and move his chair closer to mine. I suddenly felt claustrophobic as Tyrone closed in on me to my right. I quickly considered my choices: leave the O.T. session and possibly prolong my interminable stay on the unit, or move closer to William on my left, who felt non-threatening but who rarely bathed and reeked of stale alcohol, dirty clothes, and decades of sleeping on the streets of San Francisco. In the end, panic overtook me, and I completely froze. I could hear Alex talking with Mary about lacrosse in the distant background, but it was impossible to concentrate as my lungs constricted and my heart thudded and pounded so loudly it sounded as if the beating was coming from my ears. I took shallow breaths in and out and tried to steady myself to stand up and leave the room. Just as I felt strong enough to stand up, Mary called on Tyrone, and he proudly turned his paper to face the group, which was covered in multi-colored scribbles. When Mary asked him to describe his drawings, he just groaned.

As Tyrone made random noises, a new option for personal space quickly appeared in my consciousness and I moved my chair backwards, away from the group; instantaneously, I felt better and relieved. After a few deep breaths, my focus returned, and I realized that the session was over and I saw that Tyrone had moved to the couch, and the rest of my fellow patients shuffled out of the room, one by one in their purple scrubs.

NINETEEN

As I ambled out of the Day Room, I couldn't help but look across the hallway, straight ahead into Tiffany's room. Her bed was empty and unmade, and she was nowhere to be seen. There was also the addition of a neon orange sticker outside of her door, with the words *HIGH ALERT* scribbled on it; my stomach dropped, and instantly, I felt afraid. I yearned for the security of my room, which was at the other end of the hallway and a safe distance from her. I walked as quickly as I could in my slipper socks, but they proved no match for the freshly polished hallway, and I began to slide. I used all my strength to steady myself, and that's when I heard her.

- I WANT MY CHIHUAHUA! SHE'S A GODDAMN SERVICE ANIMAL! GIVE ME THE LIVERMORE SPCA NOW! Tiffany screamed into the ancient rotary phone, which did not dial or connect to any outside telephone line, repeating the appeals for her dog and occasionally demanding more Adderall.

Panic overtook me, and I stood completely still, for I knew that I had to walk past her to get to my room, which felt like the only safe place on the unit. I took a deep breath and gingerly took steps forward, not wanting to call attention to myself and risk an interaction with Tiffany, who continued to rant and rave into the phone. I found it odd that the nurses at their station, who were incredibly close to Tiffany in the distance and well within earshot of her yelling, chose to ignore her.

Just as I was about to walk through the open door of the room I shared with Jamie, something on the opposite side of the hallway caught my eye; it appeared to be light refracting from a piece of metal. My eyes blinked instinctively out of protection as the overhead lighting caused the shards of light to bounce around the hallway. I moved closer to the source of the refracting light; it was coming from a grated metal panel on the outside of a door, complete with a very austere and heavy lock. A mixture of terror and curiosity overtook me, and my body moved closer to the door, even though I felt a terrible sense of foreboding. *NO, NO, NO!* reverberated in my consciousness, and as I peered through the space between the tiny metal panels, I saw it: an extremely small room without a window or bathroom, which housed a single bed covered in a white sheet. Dark gray restraints with large metal buckles and many tightly fitting belts sprung out from the underside of the bed. The walls were cream-colored, and from my vantage point, they looked puffy and padded; I also noticed a large camera perched in the upper right-hand corner of the room. Shivers shot down my spine as I imagined the horrors and atrocities that had taken place in this minuscule room, located just a few footsteps away from the safety of my own bed.

TWENTY

- DO YOU HAVE NIGHT *BLINDNESS, A BLINDNESS* THAT ONLY COMES AT *NIGHT*?

Miss Lily loudly posed this question to me in her slow, Southern drawl, as if she were a character in a Tennessee Williams play. The hallway was her stage, and the blazing, fluorescent lights illuminated her small, skeletal frame; I could tell that at one time, Miss Lily had been a great beauty, but now she was merely a wilted flower. Her alabaster skin was full of deep wrinkles and sunspots, and her green eyes squinted at me from underneath her brown wig, styled in old-fashioned curls. Her pursed lips were covered in a garish shade of cardinal red lipstick, which only enhanced the splattering of smoker's lines surrounding them. Miss Lily wore deep blue and purple-toned galaxy-printed leggings underneath her salmon pink nightgown; the combination of colors and patterns jarred my senses, and as I stood facing her in the deserted hallway, I almost choked from her stench: she reeked of stale and extremely pungent body odor, perspiration, and urine.

- DO YOU HAVE A *BLINDNESS* THAT ONLY COMES AT *NIGHT*? Miss Lily repeated her question as I stood in the desolate hallway, trying desperately to make eye contact with the nurse who stood at a safe distance behind Miss Lily.

- What do you mean, Miss Lily? Do you mean you can't see at night sometimes? The rotund nurse ignored me but questioned Miss Lily in a gentle tone, unsuccessfully trying to rationalize her out of her psychosis.

I eyed the nurse's polar fleece jacket, complete with the hospital's logo, with jealousy: if only I had an article of clothing like that to keep me warm. Her nametag read *Gina Reece, R.N.*, and she did not seem to notice me standing there, the only patient besides Miss Lily, shivering in the hallway in the early hours of the morning. I inched closer to my room, walking backward, for Miss Lily was getting agitated and started to pace back and forth between the nurses' station and her room, which was unlocked for once. There was something almost feral about Miss Lily, and although she was a thin wisp of a woman, I felt endangered.

- Excuse me? I summoned up all the courage that I had and miraculously, Nurse Gina recognized my presence.

She motioned for me to approach her at the nurses' station, but I stood firmly in place, as I was not going to risk getting in the way of Miss Lily and her early morning constitutional.

- Can I help you? Nurse Gina asked. The answer to this question seemed self-evident, but I was polite in return: I had an agenda.

- I've been up all night; can I please have my sleeping pill? I tried to coerce a sleeping pill from Nurse Gina, for I was desperate for rest.

- *NIGHT BLINDNESS! A BLINDNESS* THAT ONLY COMES AT *NIGHT!* Miss Lily was getting more agitated by the minute and was frantically twirling around the hallway. Once again, Nurse Gina ignored me as she tended to her.

- Now, Miss Lily, please calm down. I don't want to have to put you back into your room, do I? Miss Lily recognized the threat instantly, and she stood in one place, quietly mumbling to herself.

- What is it that you need? Nurse Gina looked at me with slight hesitation and a bit of confusion and annoyance.

- Can I have my sleeping pill? The doctor said I could have 50mg of Trazadone...that's what I take at home, and I haven't had any rest since I've been here. I'm just so tired, and I...

I continued to ramble and beg for my medication as exhaustion and desperation overtook me. Nurse Gina did not immediately answer me, but she craned her neck to see the gigantic clock hanging on the wall to her right.

- It's 3:04am, just past the cut off. I can't give it to you. She stated this fact with such firmness in her voice, that I was taken aback.

I knew that there was no point in arguing, so I swiftly turned around, my back facing Nurse Gina. I quickly walked back to my room as anger bubbled and coursed through my veins; I turned down the sleeping pill offered to me only hours before, and now I found myself immensely frustrated with this decision. I had been petrified that another patient - not my roommate Jamie - would attack me in my sleep, and I felt the need to stay alert to keep watch should this occur in between safety checks. Trazadone would have instantly put me to sleep and foiled my plan to stay on guard throughout the night.

THE LIGHTS FLICKERED on and off in the dining room as the wind howled outside and rain pelted down on the windows, sullied with grime and dirt and foggy with condensation. The ambiance made me nervous as I stared at my breakfast tray and felt immediately queasy at the thought of consuming rubbery scrambled eggs, burnt gluten-free toast, and watered-down orange juice out of a cheap, plastic container. I drank two cups of decaf coffee, though, desperate for any amount of caffeine, anything to take the edge off another night plagued with insomnia and fear.

I could feel Tiffany eyeing my orange juice from across the table, but I silently refused to give it to her, as I was terrified of her temper and vowed not to interact with her. Lauren sat next to me, to my right; she shook and mumbled under her breath as all her attention was focused on opening the tinfoil that prevented her from consuming her morning yogurt. I wanted to offer to help Lauren, but I felt that I might inadvertently embarrass her, so I sat on my chair silently and looked around the dining room. William sat to my left, and I could not help but stare at his bulbous, red nose as he wolfed down everything on his plate with minimal chewing. Quite a few new faces appeared overnight, and just as I was observing them, Tyrone charged into the dining room. Even Rosa, the dining room attendant, looked up from her phone when he whizzed past her as his extremely small hospital gown flapped open, and his buttocks hung out for all to see. Tyrone was not bothered by this, as he was solely focused on consuming his breakfast, which sat on a tray next to Tiffany. His orange juice was missing, as Tiffany drank it almost thirty minutes before his whirlwind of an entry into the dining room.

Tyrone pulled out his chair with such force and noise that Rosa was forced to abandon her phone once again; she and I looked up at the same time, and we witnessed his humiliation together, as none of the other patients noticed his dynamic entrance. Tyrone was so desperate for his breakfast that he paused to take a deep inhalation before he bent his knees and plopped down on the shoddy wooden chair with all his might; his massive girth hit the chair with such force that it caused the cheap planks of wood to immediately break in half. Splinters flew around the room as the chair crumpled under Tyrone's weight; he landed on the dining room floor, encircled by shards of broken wood. Every cell in my body instantly flooded with empathy for Tyrone; I felt sorry for him and could only imagine the embarrassment he was feeling.

Something about Tyrone's situation triggered memories from my past, and I sadly recalled the pain of being an overweight child and the abuse and constant jeers of my classmates, the diets and exercise programs I was forced to try, and the shame that I constantly felt, as if something was inherently wrong with me because I was bigger than other kids my age. The worst parts of my childhood were the veiled concerns of family members, who were clearly disgusted by my appearance and openly judging me. I felt like the sole heavy person drowning amidst a sea of thin people.

During my teenage years, I struggled with anorexia and bulimia, dropping to an emaciated weight of one hundred pounds, which was tiny for my five-foot-five height and medium build. The stress of college, coupled with my desire for straight A's and academic excellence, exacerbated my condition. While other kids went out and partied on Friday nights, I was often at the gym, compulsively exercising on an empty stomach or bingeing and purging alone in the dormitory bathroom. Then, the ultimate shame came when I was twenty-two, for I stopped purging, but I could not control my bingeing during a terrible depression and nervous breakdown. The result was a weight gain of almost eighty pounds.

I met Krishna after I recovered from my breakdown and started taking medication, but I was still fifty pounds overweight; this did not matter to him, for he told me repeatedly that I was beautiful on the inside and out. For the first time in my life, I felt unconditional love, and the next thing I knew, the weight melted off, and I finally had a desire to treat my body with the care it deserved.

- Tyrone! How could you do this? Now I have to clean this mess up! Rosa admonished Tyrone while simultaneously snapping me back into the present moment.

I was getting ready to stand up and help Tyrone, who was still sitting on the floor, with large planks of wood surrounding him and his legs splaying out, when he grunted and, with great effort, stood up of his own accord. Rosa continued to belittle him, and suddenly, I felt protective of Tyrone: he did not deserve the additional humiliation of Rosa's insults. It was bad enough that everyone in the dining room was staring at him, and Tiffany stood up, enjoying the show unfolding in front of her with stifled giggles. I expected Tyrone to run out of the room, embarrassed and humiliated. Instead, he scarfed down every morsel of his breakfast while standing up, seemingly without a care in the world and with his signature grin on his face.

TWENTY-ONE

What is Self-Esteem?
  Self-esteem has several possible definitions...

1. *The way you value yourself as a human being, positive or negative.*
2. *How capable you feel.*
3. *How happy you are with yourself.*
4. *Your trust in your ability to think for yourself and take the right actions.*
5. *Your confidence in your ability to learn what needs to be learned.*
6. *The degree to which you trust and respect yourself.*
7. *Expressed through thoughts, actions, and words.*

Self concept and self image are related to self-esteem:

1. *The sum of all of the information and knowledge you have about yourself.*
2. *Includes gender, name, personality, physical appearance, race, likes and dislikes, beliefs,*

values, social history, nationality, schooling, family, career, accomplishments, failures, skills, and talents.

3. Your thoughts and ideas about your self-concept & self-image influence your own self-esteem.

Characteristics of Positive Self-Esteem

* Self awareness
* Self acceptance
* Self motivation
* Inner strength
* Attitude of gratitude.
* Self trust
* Good judgment
* Ability to find happiness
* Assertiveness
* Giving and serving others
* Forgiveness

These are areas we can work on and change through our thoughts and actions.

I had to stretch my arm quite a bit to reach the lone mini pencil in the center of the day room table, but it was worth it to correct the four typos I saw on the self-esteem handout. Internally, I breathed a sigh of relief while adding the missing hyphens, as grammatical errors had secretly been my nemesis since I worked in publishing for a few years after graduating college. I scanned the document and quickly concluded that it was a bunch of rubbish; all I had to do was look at my own experiences with depression and anxiety and observe my fellow patients, for most of us, apart from Tiffany and Connie, had the same beaten down, trod upon look. We sat with our shoulders hunched over, eyes downcast, and exuded sadness with a hint of humiliation: overly positive worksheets would never heal our shame.

Nevertheless, I kept ahold of my pencil and half-heartedly attempted to complete the second worksheet given to the small group of us in the day room, although it seemed a pointless exercise. Seconds later, I gave up and simultaneously blocked out what the Occupational Therapist was saying in her customary overly enthusiastic tone; I did not bother to look around the table in observation as I usually did. Instead, I turned my head to the right and stared at the empty and barren hallway, infinitely outstretched before me like a mirage. I pondered my current circumstances: *How did I end up here? How had my life taken such a downward spiral? What began this descent into a depression so intense I tried to take my own life?* I knew the basics: I became entangled in Aurelia's 'spiritual community' and was advised by her teacher, Bodhi, that I no longer needed my medication; conveniently, he also had his intentions set on stealing the small inheritance that grandparents had generously bequeathed to me when I was twenty-four years old. This made sense, but I knew there were crucial details missing and more to the story, yet, as hard as I tried, I could not recall anything else except that Krishna had stuck by me in my darkest of days and sleepless, nightmare-filled nights.

TWENTY-TWO

Thunder rumbled in the distance, followed by a loud clapping sound; lightning struck just as Dr. Mueller appeared in my room, on cue as if he were the villain in a low-budget horror film. He sat down on Jamie's bed very carefully and narrowly avoided becoming entangled in her dirty sheets, which had been left haphazardly on her bed each morning since her arrival.

- Can I go home now? I fired this question quickly before Dr. Mueller could ask me vague questions about my wellbeing or lack thereof.

Dr. Mueller paused and took a deep breath in through his nose and exhaled through his mouth, which allowed his pannus to burst forth from the constraints of his belt and fall over his trouser waistline. He was clearly annoyed by his belly-flopping out but also by my question.

He waited until he was good and ready to answer; finally, he turned his head to look at me. I felt my stomach turn to knots and the hairs on my arm stood-on end.

- Let me ask you a question: Why are you so desperate to leave? He had a sadistic smile on his face after he posed this query to me, and I had to admit that it had caught me off guard because it seemed utterly ridiculous and bizarre. *Who would choose to stay in a psychiatric prison when the free world was only a highly secured doorway away?* Unfortunately, for me, freedom required Dr. Mueller's acquiescence, for California law stated that the psychiatrist who signed you into the hospital was the only one who could sign you out.

Dr. Mueller continued to stare at me with a look of expectation, and it was clear that he wanted an answer to his question; the sooner, the better. I burst into tears; I could no longer take the stress of this twisted game. He abruptly stood up from Jamie's bed and triumphantly turned on his heels to walk out of the room; as he approached the doorway, I saw him pause slightly, and although I was choked up and still crying, I managed to answer him. I felt like my life depended on it.

- It's so...drab in here....there's no music or art, and it's freezing. I just want to be at home where I'm safe...I'm scared of the other patients. I miss Krishna. I could not stop the babbling once I started, and I was prepared to go on when Dr. Mueller interrupted me.

- What makes your home so 'safe'? According to your file, it's where you tried to take your own life. Also, the police officer who found you noted that you wrote a will and left a rent check for May, implying that you were determined to end your life; this was not a cry for help; you had made the decision to die already. You followed through with a lethal cocktail of Xanax and alcohol. We take these sorts of actions very seriously here.

I was instantly stunned into silence and submission. *A police officer? A will? What exactly happened?* Dr. Mueller interrupted my frantic thoughts as he continued to verbally twist the knife into my already delicate and wounded psyche.

- Your home is not safe unless you are. Do you know what I mean by this, Deborah?

I sat there silently for a moment, ignoring his question and then I shuddered and turned my face away from Dr. Mueller; I wondered which one of us was truly ill.

- You are not 'safe' unless you are not a danger to yourself or others. That means taking your medication, talking to a therapist, and basics like feeding yourself, which you have not been able to do, bathing, etc. Does that make sense? The newfound softness in his voice frightened me, and I sat quietly, waiting for him to continue, as he had made it very clear from the start of this perverted interaction that he was in charge.

I nodded my head and turned to look at Dr. Mueller, who had a neutral expression on his face for once. Instantaneously, I decided to try a new tactic: I would agree with him and forego fighting in the hopes that this would soothe his ego and help me on my quest for freedom.

- Actually, I do know what you mean. I will admit that I was not in my right mind when I first came here, but now that I'm back on my meds and going to O.T., I feel fine. I can take care of myself. Krishna will be home soon, and he can help, too...

- Ah! So, you do admit it: You are not in your right mind. He began scribbling on his yellow pad of paper. Before I could interrupt him and argue that my point was to be taken in the past tense, he had the last word. I knew that my tactic had backfired, and I had inadvertently incriminated myself. However, I did not deserve the severity of his final blow.

- You know, people have tried to take their own lives on this very ward. In fact, someone killed himself in this very room. So unfortunate. He tutted and urgently walked out of the room, his cheap dress shoes making scuffing sounds down the hallway.

WAVES OF PARANOIA washed over me, and the immense progress I had made in the past few days disappeared in their wake. I could not stop thinking about the poor man who had killed himself in the very room in which I was now trapped. *How did he do it? How old was he?* I quickly scanned the room, and the only scenarios I could come up with were that he either suffocated himself to death using the thin pillow on his bed or he had used his bedsheet to create a noose from the bathroom doorknob and had hung himself.

I dry heaved and cried for this man I never knew, for I felt his struggle in every fiber of my being; perhaps he was only a child of eighteen years old who heard voices, and death was his only escape from their torment. Maybe he was immensely depressed or suffered from massive PTSD and just could not take the pain anymore. Different scenarios and circumstances of his demise swirled in my brain and left my heart thudding in my chest as beads of sweat dripped down my chest into my cleavage and tears continued to dribble down my face. *What if his ghost haunted this room? Was his apparition the source of my insomnia each night?* The barrage of terrifying thoughts pounded in my skull, mimicking the thunder outside, as my anxiety soared to heights I had not known possible until now.

TWENTY-THREE

- DEB-O-RAH! YOU HAVE A PHONE CALL!

Connie shouted this news into my room while standing in the doorway and then quickly ran away. As she rushed down the corridor of the hospital, she continued to announce the big news of my phone call to the entire psychiatric ward; like a talking bird in a children's cartoon, she chirped away.

- PHONE CALL FOR DEB-O-RAH! DEB-O-RAH'S GOT A PHONE CALL!

For once, I was grateful for Connie, for she provided a very timely distraction from the endless panic and paranoia I had been experiencing since my tormented interaction with Dr. Mueller. As I stood up from my bed, I noticed that my scrubs were soaked through with perspiration, and I scrunched up my nose as I was instantly repulsed by my own stench. I was in a daze as I made my way down past the nurses' station to the retro-style phone dangling by a curled cord.

- Hello?

I whispered this greeting, almost terrified of who was on the other end of the phone line.

- Hartung, is that you?

I exhaled my breath, which I had been tightly holding in my chest, for I immediately recognized the gentle voice on the other end; it belonged to my best friend, Alicia Cobb.

- Cobbs?

As soon as I said her name, I burst into uncontrollable tears.

- Are you ok, Hartung? I've been calling every hospital in the city looking for you. Your aunt wouldn't give me your location or phone number until today. She had some bizarre reason that no one could talk to you until day four of your, um, hospitalization. I think she said, 'the spirits' gave her this information, another one of her bullshit excuses...

I did not truly register what Alicia Cobb, whom I had always called *Cobbs* as a nickname, was telling me about Aurelia. I was taken aback by her rant and distracted by Alex zooming past me with a disturbed look on his face and Connie, who hovered a few feet from me, hanging onto every word I uttered.

- Are you still there, Hartung? Cobbs asked me in her most compassionate tone.

- I'm here, but they're listening to me.

I quietly spoke this sentence, as I was deliberately trying to prevent Connie from hearing me, and I did not want Alex to catch parts of my conversation as he whizzed past.

- Who's listening to you? What do you mean?

Cobbs was trying to mask the concern in her voice with kindness, but I could tell that she thought I was hearing voices in my head. This was one of the special aspects of our friendship: we always knew what the other was thinking.

I was having trouble concentrating on my conversation with Cobbs, and with each passing second, I felt ungrounded and more disassociated. I was broken: a crucial part of my cognition process was missing, and I became fixated and hyper-aware of the fact that my brain refused to work properly. My deepest fear was that this damage was permanent.

- Hartung, what happened?

Cobbs tried once again to engage me in conversation. I continued to cry and wiped away my tears with my left hand while my right gripped the phone tightly. It was incredibly difficult to talk while sobbing, but I did my best to muster up the courage to speak.

- I, I'm not sure...I tried asking for help, but I asked the wrong person, Aurelia. I heard a blood-curdling scream, and the next thing I knew, I woke up here. I can't remember much more, Cobbs. My brain just won't work...I'm so scared. This place is frightening...

- Oh, Hartung. I'm so sorry, my friend. When I saw you in December, you were skin and bones, and it was as if every trauma you ever experienced was haunting you. You were raw and needed so much help. I tried to intervene as much as I could, but it was so hard after I left San Francisco and came back to New York to start my new school semester. You were in such a desperate state. I'm sorry...I could have lost you... Can I ask you a question? Were you drinking?

I was barely able to mutter an answer to her question as I was taken aback by it: *how did she know?* Finally, I just told the truth: I found myself at the liquor store one day, having no recollection of how I got there. The next thing I knew, I bought the biggest bottle of vodka I could find and began to drink straight out of the bottle as soon as I returned home. I had not had an alcoholic drink in over ten years because it interfered with my medication, and I was always cautious about protecting my liver; this turn of events even surprised me.

- Yes, I randomly started drinking vodka...

Now Cobbs began to cry, and I could tell she felt like she should have done more, but in truth, there was nothing she could have done to prevent my current circumstances. Before I could attempt to comfort her, she spoke again.

- It's that stupid bastard Bodhi's fault, isn't it? I knew he was taking advantage of you, but I had no idea it would end up like this. It makes me furious!

The Cobbs that I knew, whip-smart and full of sass, was emerging once again and I was comforted by her protectiveness.

- Does Jesse know? I gingerly asked.

- Well, she's my wife, and I was so upset when I heard the news...I had to tell her. Is that ok? Cobbs queried.

- Yeah...she's a Pisces, too, and an artist. I know she understands...she's so sensitive like me...

I sobbed heavily into the phone until I was overcome with pure exhaustion and malaise. I could tell Cobbs was going to start speaking again, and although I was grateful for her phone call, I knew that my mind and body were currently severely limited.

- I have to go, Cobbs. He's back.

Thankfully, Connie had disappeared, but Alex's pace intensified, and he almost brushed into my arm as he continued to walk up and down the hallway. I jumped backwards and tried to avoid his touch at all costs. I was so frazzled by Alex's proximity to me that I inadvertently hung up on Cobbs and hurried back to my room, which felt more unsafe than ever before. Nevertheless, my body, mind, and spirit could no longer sustain the high-intensity state of panic in which I perpetually found myself; my energy plummeted, and I quickly fell asleep on top of my sweat-drenched bed.

- DO YOU KNOW WHERE YOU ARE? CAN YOU
HEAR ME? DO YOU KNOW WHERE YOU ARE?
CAN YOU HEAR ME?

I heard these questions infiltrating my dream, a
woman's voice yelling them repeatedly from afar. Eventually, they woke me up from my exhaustion-fueled slumber.

- DO YOU KNOW WHERE YOU ARE? CAN YOU
HEAR ME? HELLO! WHAT'S YOUR NAME?

The woman's voice was shrill, and she was almost
screaming at this point as I groggily realized that she was
not part of an intrusive dream. I was still half asleep, but as
my brain slowly awoke, so too did my anxiety: my heart
began to pound and throb in my chest. I tiptoed from my
bed and the darkness of my room as the rain made a slight
tapping sound on the window and continued to keep the
sun in shadow into the blinding fluorescent light of the hallway. Before my eyes had a chance to fully adjust to the
bright light, I saw her: an older Asian woman, maybe
seventy years old, emaciated with a shock of thinning, white
hair going down the back of her tiny frame. She was
completely and utterly catatonic; her eyes did not move or
blink, and I instantly felt that she was terrified and reliving
some sort of horror in the hollows of her mind as she sat
stiffly in her wheelchair. At this point, my foggy brain
finally made the connection that the woman's voice from
my dream belonged to the patient's extremely concerned
doctor.

- WHAT'S YOUR NAME? ARE YOU EXPERI-
ENCING THOUGHTS OF SELF-HARM?

Dr. Kim's voice became even more high-pitched, and
she squatted down so that she was at eye level with her
patient. She began to speak to her in an Asian dialect,
which I thought might be Korean. No response. Instantly,
Dr. Kim switched languages and I instantly recognized

Japanese. Still no response from her patient. Finally, she fruitlessly tried to converse with her in what I guessed was Vietnamese before mumbling *Jane Doe* to herself and furiously writing on the papers she held in her hand and eventually wheeling her down the hallway into her room. I had the haunting feeling that I used to speak a foreign language, but no matter how hard I tried, I could not recall which language it was. Normally, I would have been bowled over by Dr. Kim's linguistic skills and would have been mesmerized by her talent; however, there was no time for that today. I stoically stood in the hallway and heard myself audibly gasp when she pushed the new patient's wheelchair into Tiffany's room. My limbs stiffened, and I froze with fear on my fellow patient's behalf: she was not going to be safe in that room. Tiffany was a very troubled and mentally ill person, which caused her to be volatile and dangerous; I feared for the new patient, who seemed fragile at best, and I hoped that she would not be harmed.

TWENTY-FOUR

- I'm sorry I couldn't visit you yesterday. I really had to ground myself, so I went to Muir Woods to be with the redwood trees. You know, this city is very dense.

As Aurelia prattled on about the healing vibration of trees, I realized that her absence yesterday went completely unnoticed by me, and if anything, it came as a relief. Now that I was back in her presence, sitting in the empty and dimly lit dining room, I felt waves of anxiety crash over me as my heart went *thud, thud, thud* in my ever-tightening chest, and my lungs struggled for sufficient air. Although panic was rising in my system, I felt something strange happen in my mind: it became clear and focused for the first time in almost a year.

- I'm sure you know this already, but most mental illnesses are caused by energetic attachments. I really think you should be bathing at least once a day to clear any extra attachments from yourself.

Aurelia looked directly at me after stating her case, clearly expecting me to meekly agree with her. Instead, I sat there in silent defiance, and I felt a chill run down my arms as I studied her eyes: they were a very pale, sky blue with flecks of gold around her irises; although pretty in color, they were small for her face and were encased by deep wrinkles on all sides. I almost gasped aloud as I gazed into them and saw the truth for myself: they gleamed with malice.

- Showers really do clear energy and connect you to your divine state of cleanliness. I really think you need to work on this...you'll feel better once you're clean. Plus, who wants any of the attachments from this place? Have you seen the guy pacing the halls? Everyone here is looney!

I wanted to scream, I'M ONE OF THEM, TOO! as loudly as I could. I was no better or worse than Alex or anyone else on the unit; although our symptoms manifested in different ways, we suffered from the same illness invisible to the naked eye: unbalanced brain chemistry. Furthermore, we were being held in a psychiatric unit against our free will and receiving the bare minimum of care without therapy or proper medical intervention. I had seen enough in my tenure on the psych ward to glean that most patients were given medication as a stabilizer, and then after they were fed for a day or two, they were released back into the world without any true resources, only to reappear in a few days, weeks or a month later with the same – or worse – mental health issues. We were largely misunderstood and judged by society. I wanted to scold Aurelia for being so awful and hypocritical, but instead, I selfishly used the moment for my own potential escape.

- If it's so terrible here and everyone is crazy, then why can't I go somewhere else? Somewhere private? I will pay... all I need is for you to agree and sign the papers. I continued to plead my case before Aurelia, who refused to make eye contact with me and stared straight ahead at the blank wall as if she was only half listening to me. My stomach dropped, as I could tell that she was only biding her time before another torrent of New Age babble spurted forth from her pursed and heavily lined lips.

- If you would have followed Bodhi's teachings, none of this would have happened. I've seen you fail to follow through on other spiritual lessons before, and I've held my tongue, but this time, you've really created a mess for yourself.

Aurelia swiveled her neck to look at me after making her proclamation; I thought she was finished, but she had one final blow to deliver.

- You will stay exactly where you are and reap what you've sown.

Her tone was icy and firm, and as she sat next to me, squinting her eyes to emphasize her point, I felt my blood run cold. *Reap what you've sown. Reap what you've sown.* I knew this was a common phrase, but I also knew that Bodhi used it repeatedly, with bizarre karmic implications thrown in for dramatic effect. It illustrated the firm grasp he had over my aunt; I shrugged my shoulders up, almost to my ears, and shivered. A part of me knew that it was a fruitless endeavor, but I knew I had to speak up for myself, even if Aurelia was deaf to my warning cries about her spiritual teacher, who became more sinister with each passing moment.

- If I had followed his 'teachings,' I would be dead right now.

I said it: the truth. It was supposedly going to set me free (metaphorically speaking), but physically, I still found myself trapped in a psych ward, and although I felt a tiny bit of relief after revealing this revelatory information to my aunt, not much else changed in my psyche. It took an incredible amount of willpower to speak the words that now resounded in my head and hung heavily in the air, but my effort was met with a dubious expression from Aurelia and stony silence. She petulantly wrapped her lower lip around her top lip, which I knew was her form of pouting; the wrinkles on her lips were now smooth, and she sat there with her arms wrapped around herself like a toddler, slowly rocking back and forth.

- Are you ok? Although I was the one in the hospital, I felt a momentary concern for Aurelia, for she looked, and was acting, incredibly strange.

- I'm fine. I'm just doing what I need to do to protect myself.

She snapped and turned to look at me with hatred burning in her eyes. It was clear that she meant to say, *I'm fine. I'm just doing what I need to do to protect myself FROM YOU!*

I nervously laughed out loud; of course, it was all my fault, and Bodhi was immediately absolved of his guilt and role in my attempted suicide. Why had I bothered confiding in her? She was obviously too brainwashed by Bodhi to listen to reason; if my suspicions were right, he was probably 'guiding' her through channeling sessions and tarot readings about my treatment and hospitalization; he was always there, in the background, pulling the strings of her person – and her wallet.

TWENTY-FIVE

As I slowly made my way back to my room, completely drained from my interaction with Aurelia, I passed Tiffany's room and felt terrified: the door was open, and she was pacing up and down the narrow room like an angry tiger in an enclosure at the zoo, ranting and raving about her chihuahua and Adderall, while her poor roommate sat on her bed, completely frozen and staring at the blank wall. Her eyes refused to blink, and I could tell that she was still trapped in the terror of her own psyche.

Then, out of the corner of my eye, I noticed a billboard nailed to the wall halfway between Tiffany's room and mine. It contained an elaborate table, with *Today's Date is April 11th!* Written on the top in bright green marker was a list of all the patients and their corresponding room numbers, doctors, and psychiatric nurses. *Had this been here all along?* Something about the date jarred me to my core: it was not that it verified my suspicion that I had been on the unit for four days, but something else. I stood in the hallway and stared at the date again, willing the information floating in my brain to avail itself to me and begging my neurotransmitters to fire. I tightly closed my eyes and repeated the date out loud over and over; at this point, I doubted any of the staff would bat an eyelash if I suddenly began having conversations with myself. Suddenly, a tangible source of energy ran through my entire being as the mystery was instantly solved: Krishna returned home from India on April 14th – only three days from now! They had to release me once he was home; I knew he would be my advocate and do everything he could to transfer me to a private facility or simply take me back to our apartment, which was what I needed the most. I felt stable - aside from the stress of being in the hospital - after being on my meds for just four days, and I silently vowed to take them for the rest of my life. I spun on my heels and made my way across the hallway to the Nurses' Station, determined to share this news with Dr. Mueller, for even he could not argue that I would be ready to leave soon and no longer was a danger to myself. Surely, someone else was in desperate need of my bed.

I walked as quickly as I could to the Nurses' Station, and without even observing the nurse seated before me, I began gushing about Krishna and his imminent return and the fact that he would take care of me. I emphasized that there must be another person in dire need of my bed and that I was stable, so there was no need to keep me in the hospital any longer. When I finally finished my tirade, I looked up to find Cranky Nurse staring at her computer screen, as per usual.

- Well? I pleaded.

- Well, what? She retorted.

- Can I talk to Dr. Mueller about my discharge?

Now I was beginning to worry, as it was clear Cranky Nurse had not heard a word of my passionate speech, or if she had, she did not care in the slightest about helping me.

- I'll see what I can do. Dr. Mueller is very busy today, and he will be off the entire weekend.

With that, she returned to her screen and ignored me while I hovered around her and fidgeted with my hands out of nervous habit. I was just about to give up when she finally looked up at me; I was filled with immense amounts of hope, and I waited with bated breath for her to speak.

- By the way, you have a phone call. That was it. She did not make eye contact with me and seemed to be very annoyed by my presence. Before she could inform me that she was transferring my call, I was already in front of the hideous yellowish, green rotary phone.

- Debster? A man's gentle voice, calling me by my childhood nickname.

I was shocked: it was my Dad on the line.

- Dad? Is that you?

Although I knew it was him, I was a bit doubtful. Maybe this was another illusion, or I had suffered a final break from reality. He was the last person I expected to call me, as I had been so distant towards my parents over the last year. It began, of course, with Bodhi blaming my parents for 'a traumatic event' that occurred when I was an infant (conveniently, I was too young to remember this), but then Aurelia became involved and said she witnessed my mistreatment firsthand, for she was always eager to pit me against my parents and drag me deeper into her New Age 'soul family.' None of that mattered now, and I felt the lies and illusions of the last year wash away as I was comforted by my Dad's concern.

- I'm here. So is Mom.

I burst into tears and apologized for the last year again. I said I was sorry for being so isolated and removed and that I never meant to hurt them; as guilt began to rise in my consciousness and internally, I felt the torrent of paranoia and brain fog instantly return.

- It's ok, Debster. We know you were off your medication. You must promise to take it from now on, ok?

I silently nodded my head in agreement and vowed again to take Cymbalta each and every day of my life.

- Are they...treating you alright?

My Mom's voice was wavering, and I knew this was a sign of intense worry and anxiety on her part.

- Yeah, I'm ok...I just...really want to get out of here.

This time, I was hysterically crying, and my parents tried to be soothing, although this was difficult over the telephone.

- Aurelia just called us this morning and explained what happened. We would have called sooner, but we had no idea where you were. I don't know why she didn't call us when you were in the emergency room; we're your parents, for god's sake!

I could tell my Dad was angered by Aurelia's actions, as was I. I assumed that my parents wanted nothing to do with me because I had avoided them for the better part of a year; this fact, compounded by the massive amounts of guilt Aurelia instilled into me, only made me feel more helpless and untethered from reality. The fact that my parents were clueless about my hospitalization was a shock; I knew Aurelia was manipulative, but this was a new low, even for her.

- Do you need us? We'll get on a plane today if you want.

I sighed and felt a surge of anguish and disbelief: this was the help that I had been hoping for since my admittance into the hospital, and yet, I knew that I could not accept it. I felt my emotional body being torn into shreds, and I began to shake; I knew that my aging parents always traveled together and that the sight of me in this institution would disturb my Mom to her core. It seemed unfair of me to cause her more anxiety and sleepless nights; I felt protective of her, and I was more concerned for her emotional well-being than my own.

- Thank you, but it's ok...

I fought back the tears welling up in my eyes and tried to control my quivering upper lip.

- What about when you're released? You will need some help then. Mom told me Krishna has to go back to work as soon as he gets home.

- Ok, um, that sounds good. Thank you.

I was grateful for their support, and I realized that they were right: I would need help upon my release, as I had not functioned in the world for almost a year.

- Can you ask Dr. Mueller when I will be released?

I pleaded and willed my parents to answer emphatically, 'Yes!'

- We tried, but he won't tell us anything because that sister of mine is your medical power of attorney.

My mom was clearly frustrated with this news, and so was I. *How had Aurelia managed to become my medical power of attorney?* I had no recollection of signing any documents over to her, and I thought that because Krishna was out of the country, my parents were automatically given that role, as they were my next of kin. Again, something was very wrong with this situation. I felt bile rise up in my throat, and my whole body broke out into a cold sweat as my heart pounded away in my chest.

My mom now tried to make light, small talk during my silence.

- What do you do all day? Can you at least watch TV for entertainment?

- We don't really do anything...there is a television, but it's permanently stuck on the Weather Channel.

My parents laughed simultaneously, and I felt some

relief as I inwardly recognized how absurd this was, and I was glad for a moment of amusement. I saw Dr. Mueller out of the corner of my eye, and I knew this was my opportunity to track him down and share the news of Krishna's imminent return.

- I...uh...I have to go now.

- Ok, we will call you tomorrow. Take care, Debster. My Dad hung up his telephone, but my Mom remained on the line.

- Talk to you tomorrow! Lots of love. My Mom hesitated before hanging up, but finally I heard the familiar sound of a pulsating dial tone in my ear.

I was comforted by my parents' phone call, and this seemed to be just the confidence boost I needed to confront Dr. Mueller. I used all the focus I could muster to keep my eyes on Dr. Mueller and his whereabouts; I was not going to let this opportunity go. He was standing at the Nurses' Station and talking to Cranky Nurse; he seemed to be looking through a stack of files. I walked as quickly as possible across the hallway, and just as I was about to call his name, I heard someone calling mine.

- Deb! Deb!

I cringed, as I had never liked this nickname, but I recognized Lauren's shaky voice instantly, and I knew this was her way of conveying that she liked me. I had to make an immediate choice: turn around and engage with Lauren and lose sight of Dr. Mueller and relinquish my chance to speak to him until Monday, or be a decent human being and interact with the one person who had shown me immense kindness during my time on the unit, especially when I was terrified and very confused during the first two days of my stay. When I heard Lauren's slipper socks dragging on the floor and picking up momentum behind me, I knew that my choice had been made. I sighed deeply and turned to meet my fellow patient.

- Tomorrow's pet therapy!

Lauren was quite excited to relay this information to me, and I forced myself to be energetic in return. I noticed that she looked much better than when I first met her, and she seemed steadier on her feet. Lauren's eyes were focused intently on me, awaiting my response.

- That sounds fun! How does it work? I feigned happiness on Lauren's behalf and forced myself to join the conversation.

- Lenny is coming tomorrow! He's my favorite – he's a golden retriever and his owner brings him into the Day Room for the entire morning.

Lauren was practically beaming as she continued to explain the basics of pet therapy to me; her excitement was contagious, and I sincerely began to look forward to Lenny's arrival. I had always loved animals, and I especially loved large, friendly golden retrievers. My heartstrings ached for a moment, though, as I once again thought of Lucky, the dog I walked each morning. I hoped that his owners would forgive me for not showing up to work and that I could resume my duties once I was out of the hospital.

- That sounds fun; I love dogs, especially golden retrievers.

- Me too!

Lauren smiled at me again but quickly became distracted and averted her eyes.

- I, um, have to go now. The nurse is waving at me.

Cranky Nurse struck again; I could feel it in my bones. I craned my neck towards the Nurses' Station to confirm this notion, and I saw her motioning for Lauren to join her; everything about her hand movement screamed 'NOW.' Instantly, gloom appeared across Lauren's face, and once again, she moved like a nervous and doddery old woman as she shook with each step. Her slipper socks squeaked against the smooth floor, and when Lauren finally made it to the Nurses' Station, a finger admonished her, and she was given a handful of pills in a paper cup, along with another miniature cup full of water. Poor Lauren stood there, looking guilty and afraid of Cranky Nurse, who was solely focused on Lauren's throat as she swallowed an enormous number of pills in one fell swoop.

TWENTY-SIX

- You should have seen the way they stormed into my shop and demanded the keys to your apartment! The nerve of them, the attitude – they were so fucking *demanding!*

The fatigue and systemic pain I felt weighing my body down instantly vanished when I heard my dear friend Susan swear; she was one of the kindest and gentlest souls I had ever met, and this was extremely out of character for her. The words rang through my head as I wondered who Aurelia had insisted come to San Francisco for spiritual backup. My body was on high alert again as we sat in the deserted dining room, where the evening's meal was scarfed quickly and unceremoniously by my fellow patients only thirty minutes before; I tried to piece together the impetus of her anger.

- Sorry, honey, let me back up a minute. I know this is a lot to take in. I'm sorry I couldn't visit you sooner, but I had too many shoes to get out the door this week.

- How are you feeling, my dear? Susan queried with her signature calming voice and looked at me with her hazel eyes, which emulated compassion.

I wanted to tell Susan that I was fine, but I was not able

to speak; I was overwhelmed with exhaustion, and a fuzzy mind overtook me; all I could do was hide my face in my hands. It suddenly felt very late in the evening, and I yearned to close my eyes and lie down, even if it meant sleeping on a urine-stained single bed.

- Honeybunch, are you ok? Susan moved from across the table and was instantly by my side; I could smell the citrus conditioner that coated the ringlets of her long, red hair, and I detected her floral-smelling face cream, which kept her fifty-five-year-old skin youthful and plump. The familiar aromas of my friend comforted me, and I felt safe enough to lift my face up from the palm of my hands.

- Have you eaten dinner yet, honey? I told the E.R. to make sure that your gluten allergy was in your chart when you were transferred here.

Susan seemed very concerned about my eating habits, and I did not want to cause her any more stress or undue worry, but I had skipped dinner and felt nauseous most of the time.

- I wasn't hungry tonight, but the hospital has been very good about my gluten allergy. Thank you for telling them.

I stretched out my arm to show her my bracelet, which stated this in thick marker; Susan seemed impressed in return. A second later, her attention wavered, and she turned her head to face the entrance to the dining room; I heard the door creak open slowly and then quickly close. I was surprised to see Tyrone waddle into the room, his hands gripping the freezing concrete wall for balance while his sullied hospital gown flapped open at the back, as per usual. He then turned and let go of the wall and stood facing the door, which he seemed to be fixated on; Susan and I could not help but stare, and we were tense as we waited for his next movement. We did not have to wait very long, for Tyrone now had confidence oozing out of his pores and stood like a gunslinger in an old cowboy movie. In one quick motion, he lunged forward toward the door and touched the doorknob with both hands, after which he jumped backwards and squared his shoulders and turned to face his nemesis head-on, ready for another round. He repeated this again and again, with intense focus in his eyes, while his lower lip protruded, and droplets of drool dripped off it onto the collar of his dirty gown.

Eventually, our rapt attention was diverted from Tyrone's compulsive doorknob touching; Susan and I almost jumped simultaneously when her mobile phone vibrated on the table.

- Sorry, honey. Excuse me, just a minute; let me make sure everything is okay at the shop. As Susan quickly checked her voicemail, I wondered if my cell phone was in the hospital's possession or if it was still at home. I did not pine for my phone like some patients would; I was never really attached to it and preferred to take my calls on Krishna's landline. Amidst this, Tyrone stopped attacking his doorknob foe and, weary and perspiring from his exertions, he now faced me and stared: his eyes were unfocused again, but he was looking in my general direction with a large smile on his face.

Tyrone was still staring when Susan put her phone into her purse, glanced in my direction, and lowered her voice to make sure she was out of his earshot.

- I think you have an admirer, honey. Susan's eyebrows lifted as she tilted her head backwards in Tyrone's direction.

I instantly knew what she was implying, and a shot of adrenaline combined with fear rushed through my body as I realized a frightening fact: Tyrone was attracted to me, and in his deluded mind, he might even consider me his girlfriend. Tyrone was still standing behind Susan, drooling and giving me a silly smile with his shock of brilliantly white teeth bared. I averted my eyes and quickly turned my neck to face Susan.

- I didn't mean to scare you, honey, but judging by your reactions, I did just that. My apologies. Anyway, that was Officer Henry on the phone – he was calling to check on you again. He really is the sweetest police officer! He's called or texted me every day since your incident to make sure that you're okay. When you're released, I can give you his number – just in case you would like to thank him.

My mind swirled and did mental gymnastics to no avail; I could not grasp that Officer Henry saved my life, as I could barely understand my current circumstances, let alone have perspective regarding the catastrophic events of my recent past. I had heard something about a police officer before, but I struggled to remember any details of his involvement. I assumed that it was Officer Henry who put me on a 5150, a psychiatric hold in the state of California. I looked at Susan questioningly, and I silently thought, *Who is Officer Henry? Why would I want to thank the person who put me in this horrible place?*

- It's not like that, honey. Susan seemed to be reading my mind, and I noticed that her beautiful porcelain-colored skin with freckles scattered about turned to a shade of white.

- You really can't remember anything, can you? Susan calmly asked me this question, but there seemed to be fear in her eyes as she looked directly at me and then craned her neck to see Tyrone still standing behind us, lips hanging open with dried spittle on them and his eyes looking in my general direction.

Tyrone quickly faded into the background of the stark white dining room wall as I tried to focus my attention on Susan. I desperately wanted to tell her that fragments of my attempted suicide pierced through my psyche at random and caused immense amounts of stress, sadness, and even hysteria. I yearned to share with her that the last thing I remembered was that I was standing alone in my kitchen, and I felt the entire weight of the last year's depression and traumas; I finally pieced together that I was being controlled by Bodhi and at the time I was desperate for an escape from his manipulation and the relentless emotional pain I was experiencing. A part of me felt as if death was the only way to be freed from Bodhi's clutches, yet there was still a glimmer of hope in my mind when I made my final telephone call for help. Unfortunately, I almost instantly heard the phone's dial tone, and I let out a blood-curdling scream, which encased me and felt like it was coming towards me from all directions at once, building momentum until it's suffocating crescendo and then; absolute darkness. I could not put these thoughts into words, though, and my mouth was suddenly frozen again; goosebumps appeared on my arms as I had the realization that the scream I heard was my own. I was bewildered: how could such a guttural, purely animalistic sound build momentum in my lungs and escape through my mouth? I barely raised my voice, even when I was angry, and this horrifying sound haunted me as it replayed itself in my mind; I knew it would terrorize me for the rest of my life.

- DEBBIE? Dear Debbie, are you still with me? Susan's voice was strained, and I could sense genuine concern in her actions, words, and intense eye contact. She held onto my right arm and squeezed it quite hard. Although this was uncomfortable, it brought me back from my flashback and into the present moment.

I had a terrible, pounding headache, and my mouth felt

dry and as if it was full of cotton; I had trouble swallowing and felt queasy as my mouth eventually filled with saliva. Finally, I was able to swallow and speak.

- I'm here...I just had a –

- It's ok, dear, I know. Susan loosened her grip on my arm and gave it a few pats before she removed her hand.

I was confused and shaken, but a question loomed in my brain, and being: it was all I could think of: *Who was I speaking to on the phone? Did someone hang up on me during a cry for help?* I was overcome with a sense of foreboding, and I looked at Susan with desperation in my eyes, almost pleading with her for answers.

- Well, my dear, I can tell that you need some answers and someone to help you put the puzzle pieces together. I will try my best to help. I nodded my head and silently willed Susan to continue.

- You were speaking with Aurelia, and this is just my opinion, honey, but it looks like you just hit the call button in desperation, and your phone automatically called the last person you were speaking to. Does this sound about right?

- Yes. It took immense amounts of strength to focus my concentration on speaking just one word. I could not help but hang my head in sadness; as I did this, I noticed that my hands were shaking quite badly.

- You called Aurelia in a very...um, *precarious* state of mind. You clearly needed someone to help you, but she was not that person, honey. She hung up on you to avoid getting you involved with the "western medical system," as she called it, and instead phoned me. I barely know her, but for some reason, she had my number saved on her phone because we went on a retreat together a few years ago – you remember? Anyway, her actions were completely nonsensical, my dear, but it's the truth. During this time, honey is when you took the bottles of pills and drank an awful lot of vodka. You must have stumbled in your kitchen and bumped into your cabinet because your wine glasses fell and were found in pieces on the floor. Somehow, you miraculously made it to your living room, which is where I found you passed out. Wait, one more detail that I forgot to mention: as soon as I heard from that crazy aunt of yours, I closed the shop and sped over to your apartment; there was no answer on your phone, and obviously, you could not come to the door to let me in. I called 911, fearing the worst.

Susan paused to take a breath, and I could tell that these memories were causing her pain, which she valiantly tried to hide from me. I felt ashamed that I had caused one of my best friends so much stress and emotional turmoil, but with a hunger and desperation I had never experienced before, with every fiber of my being, I needed to know how the rest of the story unfolded. I blinked my eyes and nodded my head so that she could continue uninterrupted.

- The firetruck arrived first, but because you were stuck in your apartment, there was nothing for the firemen to do, so they just waited outside. Then Officer Henry arrived, and honey, I swear he's an angel incarnate. Anyway, Officer Henry could not enter your building or break down the door to your apartment because he didn't have a warrant. He did notice that the windows in your living room were open, and although it was against police protocol, he borrowed a long ladder from the firetruck, climbed up to your apartment, and entered the living room through one of the large open windows. He called for an ambulance immediately and then let me into the building. The amazing part of it all was that none of your neighbors saw a thing! Usually, people are outside gawking in these situations, but I think because it was the middle of the week during the day, everyone was at work. The only downside of this miraculous rescue was that because it took quite a bit of time, the Emergency Room doctor could not pump your stomach because of the half-life of Xanax, so she just gave you fluids -

Susan continued to speak, but it was impossible for me to completely focus, as I was overwhelmed and oversaturated. Tears welled up in my eyes, and my body began to shake violently; I felt sick to my stomach as foul-tasting bile burned my throat when unexpectedly, a crystal-clear thought entered my mind: *The doctor could not pump my stomach; this must be part of the reason I feel so ill.* Susan was still speaking to me, this time in a very soothing voice, but I could not understand a word of what she said: it was as if she was speaking in gibberish or some strange tongue. I felt like my heart would explode from pounding so intensely in my chest, and I almost jumped out of my chair when the door to the dining room loudly opened.

- Visiting hours have been over for twenty minutes! Deborah, you know the rules – it's time for bed. Tyrone! What are you doing in here? Come with me right now; it's time for your sleeping pill. The last things that I heard were Tyrone's signature shuffle and the nurse's athletic shoes squeaking quickly on the floor as they left the dining room.

WHEN I FINALLY CAME TO, it was the early hours of the morning, and as the rain gently sprinkled on the windows, I lay in my filthy bed, sweating and shaking, holding my head with my hands as I rocked back and forth uncontrollably. Somehow, even in my incredibly anxious state, I had managed to pick up key phrases from Susan as she spoke, and her voice reverberated in my consciousness as I tried to piece together what had really happened that fateful Wednesday morning.

Aurelia demanded to be your medical power of attorney when you finally woke up in the hospital.

I knew she was up to no good, and today, when she and her friend, Crystal, came into my shop uninvited and demanded keys to your apartment, it was confirmed.

Aurelia claimed that they were going to sage your apartment, but I knew they were going to snoop around and look for your will. I'm sorry to say that Bodhi was behind it all. He's still controlling Aurelia, Crystal, and God knows how many others. Over my dead body, would I let him control you again, honey!

You kept repeating Bodhi's name when you came to the hospital, and it was clear that there was a negative connotation associated with him. I just knew in my gut that he was responsible for all of this.

Officer Henry took the will and note you left by the front door to your apartment as evidence. I had the sense that something like this might happen, so I went over a few days ago, and I opened all the curtains, cleaned up the few remaining pills, liquor, and the glass in the kitchen, and put your paints away. I tried to organize your paintings, but there were so many of them, honey! Oh, I also put your pipe in the closet; I know it was just a little weed, but Aurelia and Crystal don't need to know about that! Officer Henry just pretended he didn't see the pipe.

I could not stop Susan's voice from repeating itself in my head, and with each haunting reiteration, my panic, fear, and feelings of betrayal increased; hours later, completely exhausted and spent, I fell into a fitful, dreamless slumber.

TWENTY-SEVEN

The wind outside whinnied like a horse, and the rain pelted against the window as I woke up; my scrubs were soaked through with sweat again, and I was instantly terrified. I shivered and noticed Jamie's vacant and unmade bed in the half-light of the morning, presenting itself in perfect juxtaposition as unbearably bright light streamed in through the open door to our room. My body was stiff and aching, and my head throbbed; I tried swallowing, but my mouth was incredibly dry, and even this basic bodily function proved difficult. My hands and feet tingled, and a feeling of pins and needles pulsated through my appendages. I was weak, sick, and confused; whatever slivers of clarity I had possessed in the last day, or two disappeared as something snapped during the night with my cognition process. I was left discombobulated, dirty, and unable to even begin to question what the impetus of these intense emotions was.

As I put my feet down on the ice-cold floor, I felt a stabbing pain through my arches that shot up to my toes. I was unstable as I stood up; when I tried to walk, my feet dragged more than usual, as they tingled and felt numb. My hands also possessed these strange sensations; I could move them, but I had lost a significant amount of feeling as neuropathy overtook them. Additional bursts of panic and paranoia surged through me as I stood frozen in place and trembled with fear.

TWENTY-EIGHT

I dragged myself out of my room and into the hallway with one thought on my mind: *coffee*. I could not care less that it was decaf; I craved not only the miniscule amount of caffeine on offer, but a sense of normality. I was an early riser and drank at least three cups of coffee every morning while at home, usually listening to records and enjoying the stillness and quiet outside, as the city began to awake from its nighttime slumber.

There was something different about the hallway this morning: it was a veritable ghost town, completely silent and empty, except for Nurse Jack, who sat at the Nurses' Station looking refreshed and happy, as he had clearly only just begun his shift. I was in no mood for small talk, so I tried my best to skulk by him and purposely avoided eye contact. Unfortunately, the noise of my feet dragging on the floor alerted him to my presence.

- Deborah! Good morning! Listen to this poem I just wrote; I think you will like it.

Reluctantly, I turned around and headed away from the dining room and my cup of coffee and back to the Nurses' Station, where Nurse Jack was scribbling away on a piece of paper. I was envious of his flourish of the pen, as I was tired of using miniature golf pencils to write. Finally, he looked up at me with a twinkle in his eye.

- I use my stupidity for good! Not evil! As he made this proclamation, Nurse Jack stuck his left index finger straight into the air.

This only caused more confusion on my part, and I looked at him questioningly.

- Listen to the first few lines of my poem; it's about that bloated, orange-faced conman running for president. What a joke! He will never win – the American people are not that stupid. Especially me, for I use my stupidity for good – not evil!

Once again, Nurse Jack's index finger shot up into the air as he repeated his famous line. I was utterly flummoxed; I had not read a newspaper in almost a year, and I was completely out of touch with world news and, especially, politics. I ascertained that this was an election year, but I had no idea who this mysterious candidate was.

- Listen! Are you ready? It's only the beginning, but I could use your help with the ending and a word that rhymes with 'fall.'

Nurse Jack eagerly began the recitation of his poem and I felt forced to stand and listen.

> Trumpty Dumpty built a great wall,
> From which he hoped all Mexicans would
>   fall.
> If this tax evader can run for president,
>   anyone can!

He blathered on, but I stopped listening; I had no idea what his poem was about. I eventually just turned away, desperate at this point to leave the spectral hallway and make my way to the dining room at a turtle's pace.

IT WAS another wet and miserable morning; a heavy layer of fog and plump raindrops could be seen from the dining room windows. I ignored the plethora of new faces eating breakfast and purposely sat down on a cold, plastic seat to my left that was vacant. I procured my decaf coffee, and although my hands were tingling, I managed to grip the mint green plastic mug and gingerly sip from it. I did not care that the coffee was lukewarm and bitter; for a brief instant, I closed my eyes and dreamed that I was sitting on a cushion in my living room at home, safe and free.

My reverie was soon interrupted as a new patient plopped down in the once vacant seat to my left; the intensity of her weight hitting the plastic chair caused reverberations throughout the dining room table. The dregs of my coffee spilled over my scrubs, adding to their dampness. I quickly stole a look at my fellow patient, and to my surprise, I noticed that she was wearing street clothes, or rather, a lack thereof. The entirety of her legs was exposed, as was her derriere; the booty shorts she wore barely covered her ample and dimpled flesh. Her stomach burst forth from a tank top two sizes too small, and all she had covering her feet were flip-flops. I shivered in response and wondered how she could withstand the chill in the air. She was dressed for a day at the beach, not for an indefinite stay on a glacial psychiatric ward. I was curious to look at her face, as I had the feeling that she was probably in her mid-twenties and wearing a tremendous amount of makeup. Just as I was about to take another peek, Tiffany appeared. She slithered up to the new patient like a snake in waiting; suddenly,

Tiffany was extremely close to the new girl, and I could see the dirt in her faded green hair, the pimples bubbling to the surface of her oily face and smell the foul odor on her person; I silently wondered if she had bathed at all since her arrival.

- HEY, GIRL. YOU NEW HERE? Tiffany was now only centimeters away from the new patient. I curled my shoulders forward as I was feeling slightly afraid of her; I kept my eyes looking straight ahead, lest Tiffany think I was listening to her interrogating the new patient at an incredibly high decibel.

- YOU LIKE KMEL? 106.5 RADIO? R&B AND RAP? OLD SCHOOL MUSIC? After what seemed like an eternity, I heard a young girl's voice in response.

- I don't know what that is. I'm from L.A.

- C'MON, GIRL. YOU LIKE RAP MUSIC OR WHAT? Tiffany belligerently asked.

- I prefer alternative music. The new girl was polite, but I could tell she was getting frustrated with this intrusion during her breakfast.

- I MAY LOOK WHITE, BUT INSIDE I'M BLACK AS HELL, JUST LIKE YOU. MY DAD, DON, HE'S REALLY DARK. GIRL, I LOVE THAT RAP MUSIC, AND I CAN SHAKE MY BOOTY LIKE NONE OTHER.

Tiffany continued to bizarrely ingratiate herself with the new patient solely due to the color of her skin. I took this opportunity to quickly look at her wristband: *Jaclyn Jones. DOB: 07/02/87.* My suspicions were confirmed: she was very young, and I could tell that Tiffany's advances were starting to scare her. I was beginning to feel frightened as well; I was suspicious of this new side of Tiffany's personality, and I knew her feigned interest in Jaclyn was purely selfish, but I could not quite work out her motive yet.

While Tiffany prattled on and Jaclyn began to voraciously eat her breakfast beside me, my head started to throb, and I suddenly felt trapped: it was time to take my leave. I waited for a break in their conversation, and then I stood up as quietly as possible, careful not to look at Tiffany or make eye contact with her. I skulked out of the dining room and dragged myself down the empty hallway, carefully avoiding Nurse Jack. When I returned to my room, I immediately laid down on my sopping bed and closed my eyes in pure and utter exhaustion. I instinctively knew I was alone in the room – I saw Jamie in the Day Room earlier - and for once, there was a stillness and silence on the ward. This newfound silence was alarming and eerie, and it provided me little escape from the horrors of my psyche. My head pounded, and I closed my eyes; I could feel minuscule movements and pain behind my heavy eyelids. I began to fear the neuropathy in my hands and feet, and I obsessed over the cause of this new affliction.

During my visit with Susan, I gained clarity as to how I ended up on the psychiatric ward. I thought learning these cold, hard facts would quell some of my anxiety and confusion; unfortunately, it seemed to have the opposite effect, and I felt my sanity on the verge of completely snapping. I ruminated for hours over my situation, and while I grasped the logistics of how I physically ended up in the hospital, I felt like I would never fully understand why. It made sense that Aurelia would hang up on me in my moment of crisis, as she had never been able to take responsibility for her own emotions, let alone deal compassionately with someone else in distress. Yet, I yearned for an answer to a deeper question: why did Aurelia bulldoze into my life and manipulate me into getting involved with her New Age group? *Group. Cult. Group. Cult.* The words now seemed interchangeable. I felt vomit rise and burn my esophagus as I instantly knew the answer to my question: I was simply prey for her, and my involvement and money spent within Aurelia's circle raised her to a higher rank within the group. She manipulated me time and time again simply for her own gain. *How could she do this to her own flesh and blood?*

Almost as deep a betrayal as Aurelia's was that of Bodhi; I felt like a fool to have fallen for his charade. I knew I would be eternally embarrassed for allowing him to be my therapist of sorts and for sharing my deepest and darkest secrets with a fraud. I knew that I could have died or, worse, lost Krishna because I let myself be out-maneuvered by a greedy, New Age monster masquerading as some kind of spiritual savior. I could not stop criticizing and judging myself; in frustration, I started to grab the thin wisps of hair remaining on my head and scratch and pick an old scab on my head until I felt warm blood oozing onto my index finger.

TWENTY-NINE

My face was instantly covered with big, slobbery kisses as Lenny the Golden Retriever jumped onto the couch and devoted all his attention to me. Lauren moved quicker than I thought possible and was instantly by my side, petting Lenny and vying for a lick or kiss. Lenny's visit was the most exciting thing that happened on the psych ward all week, and it brought Lauren back to life as if by magic. Lenny's presence brightened her eyes, and she seemed at once content and childlike. It also gave me a much-needed respite from incessantly analyzing and criticizing myself.

Lauren and I forgot that Lenny had an owner until we heard her clear her throat in a manner that was clearly intended to divert our attention from her service dog. I reluctantly craned my neck so that I could still pet Lenny and make polite conversation with her at the same time; I looked at Lenny's owner, a mid-seventies Caucasian woman with a wiry thin frame, light brown eyes and dark brown hair with bright blonde highlights. Her skin was wrinkled and tanned; she clearly spent much of her time outdoors with Lenny. I was about to introduce myself and do my best to make polite small talk, but something about her expression held me back: she seemed bored and almost annoyed. This caused consternation on my part, as I knew that bringing a service animal onto a psychiatric ward was completely voluntary.

- I HAD A SERVICE ANIMAL, YOU KNOW! THEY TOOK HER AWAY FROM ME! SHE SHOULD BE HERE NOW!

Tiffany burst forth into the Day Room with her eyes bulging and an air of anger so intense she was almost frothing at the mouth. She shouted uncontrollably about her own service dog; she was so loud that she not only scared Lauren, Lenny's owner, and me but Lenny was clearly disturbed and whimpered in response to Tiffany's yelling.

- GIVE ME THE LIVERMORE SPCA! I WANT HER BACK!

I heard someone running down the hallway, and the next thing I knew, an older female nurse that I had never seen before appeared on Tiffany's left side and attempted to calm her down while leading her out of the room while Tiffany raged and yelled continuously.

- SHE WAS A GODDAMN CHIHUAHUA!

Lauren and I stole a glance at each other, and our eyes widened in unison; Lauren quickly began to pet Lenny's head, and he once again seemed happy and unfazed by Tiffany's outburst. I turned my body and faced Lenny's owner; she returned my gaze and looked stonily back at me without an iota of emotion on her poker face. My stomach dropped, and I knew that our time with Lenny was over. I was devastated; the watch on the right hand of Lenny's owner attested that Lauren and I had sat with Jenny for only ten minutes. We felt incredibly lucky that none of the other patients seemed interested in pet therapy, for it meant that we were the sole recipients of Lenny's undivided attention. Lenny's owner stood up and once again looked at me while making her announcement.

- Lenny had a long walk this morning. He's getting tired now, so we should go.

As she made her excuse to leave, I looked at Lenny: his tail was wagging happily back and forth, and he was cuddling with Lauren on the couch. Lenny was curled into the shape of a crescent moon, and his head lay on Lauren's right shoulder; Lauren petted Lenny's head with her left hand. Nevertheless, as soon as his owner began to walk out of the Day Room, Lenny instantly jumped off the couch and loyally trotted after her.

AFTER THE ANTICLIMACTIC and incredibly underwhelming session of pet therapy, Lauren and I silently walked out of the Day Room and headed back to our respective rooms. Lauren had an air of dejection and looked heartbroken and as if she might begin to cry; pet therapy had meant so much to her, and it had been spoiled partly by Tiffany's outburst and by the indifference and lack of caring by Lenny's owner. I watched as Lauren shuffled down the hallway; her shoulders were hunched over, and she looked like a deflated balloon.

I began to slowly walk back to my room, and I was instantly shocked by the incredible amounts of tingling and pain I felt in my hands and feet; I balled my fists up to make sure my hands still functioned, and I felt so unsteady as I walked down the hallway. I could not help but notice a large orange sticker outside of Tiffany's room that read: HIGH ALERT PATIENTS. I squinted my eyes to read the minuscule writing underneath the sticker and discovered that the room contained not one but two patients named Tiffany, both deemed to be even more threatening and dangerous than the usual patient. The door to their room was wide open, and my reading was interrupted by Tiffany Number One's voice.

- YEAH, GIRL, I HAVE TURNED A FEW TRICKS IN MY DAY. WHO SAYS I CAN'T? I'M GOOD-LOOKING ENOUGH, RIGHT? I'M A HUSTLER. THAT'S WHAT I'M GOING TO DO TO GET THE MONEY FOR THE BUS BACK TO LIVERMORE. I NEED TO GET MY GODDAMN DOG BACK!

Tiffany Number One's loud voice – almost a scream, really – echoed down the hallway, while Tiffany Number Two's voice was muffled and barely audible.

- I WAS TWEAKING FOR DAYS BEFORE I GOT HERE. I JUST NEED A FUCKING REST. I'M SO TIRED, AND THESE ASSHOLES WON'T GIVE ME ANY ADDERALL. MY OWN AUNT CALLED THE COPS ON ME – BITCH!

Tiffany Number Two was silent in response to this statement, but I imagined that she must be nodding her head in solidarity, as Tiffany Number One was a potentially harmful roommate and not to be trifled with in any way.

Tiffany Number One continued to prattle on while Tiffany Number Two refused to utter a single word. At this point, I forced my feet to work and ignored the strange half-asleep feeling that emanated from them. I quietly walked back to my room, lest one of the Tiffanys were to discover that I was eavesdropping.

Nurse Jack had vacated his post at the Nurses' Station, and the hallway was empty. As I shivered and wished for a warm sweater and heavy sweatpants, it occurred to me that the catatonic, older Asian woman who was Tiffany Number

One's original roommate had disappeared from the unit. My heart sank as I remembered that she did not have any friends or family; I feared the worst for her and hoped that she was not transferred to a state-run facility, which was rumored to be worse than jail.

THIRTY

I fell into a deep, dreamless sleep. When I awoke, I was wet from perspiration and shivering. The rain made a gentle, *thud, thud* sound on the window; my room was completely dark, except for the bright stream of artificial light beaming in from the hallway, as the door to my room had been left partially open after the most recent safety check.

I was incredibly disoriented, and I was experiencing an amplified sense of timelessness. I could have been sleeping for an hour or two days; I could not tell the difference. My eyes burned from dryness, and my body was on fire with pain from head to toe; neuropathy dominated my weak and tingly hands and feet. I fell back on the bed and curled up under the soggy blankets strewn across the bed; my eyes closed of their own accord, and my body was lethargic and heavy. I drifted off again into a seemingly endless slumber.

THIRTY-ONE

The sound of the door to my room opening and hitting the wall penetrated my nap, a sleep so sound it felt fathomless and restorative. Unless I was going to wake up in my own bed, at home with Krishna, I wished with every particle of my being that this sleep would never end.

- Deborah. DEBORAH! Time to get up.

I heard a woman's voice straining and almost yelling, and my eyes blinked open in response, only to quickly close again after being traumatized by the bewilderingly bright hospital light that now flooded my room.

- Deborah, it's almost two in the afternoon. You've missed lunch again. Everyone is in the Day Room; come join us.

My eyelids fluttered and opened once again, this time tolerating the blazing light. I saw an elderly woman of medium build, with a slightly hunched neck, standing at the foot of my bed; her skin was olive toned with deep wrinkles and sunspots, but a gentleness shone through her light brown eyes. Although the nurse was being stern and ordering me to get out of bed, I could sense that even in my hazy, half-asleep state, that she was actually a very kind person and a potential ally.

- I'm Nurse Eileen. I'm filling in this weekend during the day shift.

I nodded in response and felt the intense heaviness and stiffness of my neck and upper spine.

- Also, it's not good to isolate. You need to be with others–

- I'm not isolating. I'm just exhausted.

I was suddenly wide awake and felt a rush of adrenalin shoot through my body at what I perceived to be a criticism from Nurse Eileen. I instantly felt defensive, though it was clear that Nurse Eileen meant no harm. I was loathe to hear a bunch of psych ward babble about the downfalls of isolation, and I changed the subject quickly, as my stomach suddenly churned and growled. Although I had just met Nurse Eileen, I boldly decided to ask her for a favor.

- I'm very hungry, do you think I could have a snack?

I implored Nurse Eileen to take pity on me and let me have something to eat, although I knew it was against the rules. She raised an eyebrow and smiled in return.

- Let me see what I can do. I'll meet you in the Day Room.

Nurse Eileen quickly left my room before I could protest. I knew the snack would be a reward for socializing with my fellow psychiatric ward patients; as my belly rumbled, I decided it was a fair exchange. I slowly got out of bed and ambled towards the Day Room.

I THOUGHT for a second that my eyes were deceiving me: in the left-hand corner of the Day Room, I came face to face with a rickety, old wooden bookcase. Each shelf was filled to the brim with books, many of the spines frayed and covers tattered. I felt a flutter of excitement in my stomach overtake my hunger pains as I thought about this fortuitous discovery: Books were magical to me, and since I was a toddler, they provided me solace, escape, entertainment, and comfort. I remember reading all night with a flashlight as a child as I let my imagination run wild with stimulation. As an adult, I was constantly reading and rarely out in public without a book, as my voracious appetite for reading was insatiable. Even when I sank into deep and dark depressions, the very act of reading often became my only source of hope, my lifeline.

I tilted my head to get a better look at the spines of the books on the shelf that were eye-level to me: *Mockingjay, A Confederacy of Dunces, Ham on Rye, The Corrections, A Hundred Years of Solitude, Love in the Time of Cholera, Cat's Cradle, The Kite Runner, A Fine Balance.* Besides the first title on the list, I knew with every fiber of my being that I had read the entirety of these titles in my twenties and that each book had had a profound effect on me. I felt something eerie wash over me. It was as if Athena, the Greek goddess of wisdom, had come down from on high and placed a time-line of my life in my early twenties in book form right in front of my eyes. *For what purpose, though? What was I supposed to glean from this?* I wrapped my arms around myself as I shivered; my head spun for a minute as I tried to recall authors, plots, narratives, characters – anything to connect to the special and unique power of some of my favorite books. Frustration instantly rose as I was not able to recall any of the details I so yearned to remember. I was drawn to *A Fine Balance,* and I ran my index finger over the weathered spine, willing myself to remember the symbolism of this book in my life. Again, I drew a mental blank. I turned the book over, and without paying much attention to the cover image, I immediately glanced at the author's name: *Rohinton Mistry. Of course! How could I have forgotten this?* I opened to the first chapter, but my eyes would not cooperate with the small font, and I instantly felt the beginning of a throbbing headache. I put the book back on the shelf with a sadness in my heart; all I wanted to do was to read and be immediately transported away from my current circumstances, but my eyes simply would not focus on the text. As I stood in awe of the bookshelf and took in its musty scent, like that of a used bookstore with creaky floor-boards, I thought I heard someone calling my name. I turned around and saw Lauren sitting on a wobbly plastic chair and my roommate, Jamie, sitting across to her right in a similarly unstable plastic chair.

- Deb! We're going to play a game, wanna join us?

Lauren seemed to have recovered from the utter disap-pointment of pet therapy and had a little spark in her eyes. I was grateful for the distraction, as I was slightly unsure if what I was experiencing in front of the bookcase was real or if the single thread of sanity I possessed had finally unrav-eled. I immediately sat down in the plastic chair to Lauren's left and willed myself to play the game, whatever it was, and to stay focused and in the present moment.

Jamie sat in a chair at the head of the shoddy, makeshift coffee table; she was to my left. Lauren's trembling hands slowly moved a large, yellowed, rectangular box into the center of the table. The images on the front cover of the box were worn out decades before, but I made out *CANDY LAND* written in an enormous font that looked like twisted pieces of peppermint candy. My heart skipped a beat as I remembered that I loved playing this game as a child. Lauren made a move to remove the top of the box but then passed it to me; I understood that her hands were especially shaky today. I forced my tingling fingers to work, lifted the weathered top of the box off, and placed it on the table; after that, I suddenly froze, and I could not remember the next step to initiating the game. I was embarrassed and looked sheepishly at Jamie for help; she was very happy to take charge, and immediately, the boxes' contents were strewn across the table. There was a multi-colored board complete with a rainbow trail and cartoon characters from the fabled and magical land of sweets, including the friendly Mr. Minty, the devilish Lord Licorice, and the always jolly Princess Lolly; also present was a green plastic cut out of a gingerbread man, a silver thimble, a small silver figurine of a dog, a stack of worn-out cards with barely readable colored boxes, and a pair of dice. The directions were completely absent, and Lauren and I both looked imploringly at our silently nominated leader, Jamie.

- Let's see, I don't think we have directions, so we can just wing it today!

Jamie seemed to be in her element and for the first time since I met her, she seemed relatively happy and animated, as opposed to being elusive and brooding on the couch of the Day Room. Lauren and I were both grateful to have someone show us how to play this simplest of games, as we had big, gaping holes in our memories and the directions eluded us.

- Should we roll the dice to see who goes first?

Lauren asked this question, and it was clear that she was confused, yet I could tell that she was also excited for a diversion. Although my instinct was that the dice were in the box by mistake, I went along with her suggestion.

- Why don't you roll first?

After my suggestion, Lauren tried numerous times to pick up the dice but continued to have trouble; finally, Jamie picked them up and placed them in her hands. Lauren shook the dice with closed fists and then rolled five.

I was next, and although it was difficult for me to grip the dice, I forced myself to pick them up and took my turn: two.

- Snake eyes!

Jamie cheered on from the head of the table.

Jamie rolled a four, but rather than celebrate as she did with my results, she looked encouragingly at Lauren to begin playing the game, as she was clearly the winner of the round of dice rolling.

- Now, what do I do?

Lauren asked aloud, and I thought to myself, *good question*. I tried to will my brain to remember the rules to this child's game but, to my embarrassment, I just could not remember any clues to the workings of this overly simple game.

- Hmm, I know! We each pick a different colored gingerbread man – or, in our case, one gingerbread man and a random Monopoly dog and thimble - and then pick a card and move it along the board.

- When do we roll the dice?

Lauren queried. I was still unsure of the role of the dice, but because my memory was so fuzzy, I knew that I could be easily mistaken. I thought it best to leave things to Jamie, our fearless leader; she looked pensive for a minute as Lauren and I eagerly awaited her answer.

- I don't think we use them in this game; they must be in the box by mistake.

There was something in the tone of Jamie's voice which reminded me of a patient teacher for young children.

- Sorry to interrupt, but are you a teacher?

- How did you know? I'm a kindergarten teacher!

Jamie beamed and was clearly proud of her profession and I was grateful for her skills, which were quite useful as we whiled away some time and continued to attempt to entertain ourselves with a game.

- Now, let's shuffle the cards and begin the game.

Lauren turned toward me with a pleading look in her eyes, and I understood that there was no way she could shuffle a deck of small cards; I moved them across the table in front of Jamie, who reveled in her shuffling duties.

Jamie and I let Lauren pick a card first and she drew a blue square; we both waited patiently and silently encouraged Lauren as she tried and tried again to grip her plastic gingerbread man. Finally, she triumphed and happily moved him onto the board and to the first blue square.

- I'm so happy that we're playing this game. This hospital used to be so different - really supportive - and more like a helpful community. It's really changed a lot in the last few years.

I was touched by Lauren's genuine love of Candy Land and that this simple interaction meant so much to her. There was something she said that made me curious, and I couldn't help but wonder how many times she had been committed to this facility. As if reading my mind, she answered my question of her own accord while Jamie continued to play the game and moved her Monopoly dog onto the red square on the board.

- I've been here at least four times over the last ten years.

As Lauren confided this information to Jamie and me, I felt immense sadness on her behalf.

- It's not so bad here; at least we have clean sheets and scrubs. I've been to other hospitals in the city where the nurses play cards all day, and you have to take group show-ers. Oh! There's also a psych ward in Fremont where bras are considered 'contraband material,' and you're not allowed to wear them.

My eyes widened, and I gasped out loud.

- I know! It's really terrible, isn't it? Since when was being mentally ill a crime?

Lauren made a good point, and I continued to ponder her rhetorical question as I silently moved my Monopoly thimble to the green square. Jamie did not show any emotion on her face and continued to be intently focused on the game at hand, while Lauren and I were distracted and had completely lost our focus. Eventually, Jamie got up and left the Day Room as she was bored without an activity to focus on. Lauren and I sat next to each other in comfortable silence until Connie came into the Day Room and announced that it was snack time.

THIRTY-TWO

- I'm not really supposed to do this, but since it's the weekend and we don't have any activities planned, so I think we can watch a movie.

Nurse Eileen's silver keys jingled and jangled as she unlocked the cupboard door to the right of the television, which was still tuned to the weather channel. I stared at the forecast for the week ahead, willing bursts of sunshine to appear on the screen, but all I saw was the gloom of dark rain clouds and bolts of lightning.

- Hmmm...there's not a lot of selection here, but it looks like we can watch *Fast and the Furious One* or hmm...that's it. That's the only DVD here.

Nurse Eileen looked slightly puzzled by the limited selection of films, but no one other than me seemed to be bothered, as the promise of watching a movie, *any* movie, was a massive thrill to the average psych ward patient. I looked around the Day Room, and there were at least seven of my fellow patients sitting with rapt attention, eager for distraction and entertainment. I sat by myself, to the left of the television and in the back row, conveniently closest to the hallway, just in case I felt anxious and needed to make a quick exit. Connie was pacing around behind me, and in the front two rows in front of me sat Lauren, Jamie, Alex, Jaclyn, and Tyrone. Closest to the television was Roger, the toothless, homeless man I had not seen for days; even he felt compelled to make a special appearance for the afternoon movie.

My mood had soured, though, as the last thing I wanted to watch was a movie about men speeding around Los Angeles in fancy cars without a narrative or inspired dialogue. I thought about standing up and walking out of the Day Room, but Nurse Eileen had arranged the chairs so nicely in front of the television, and I saw her - out of the corner of my eye - putting jellybeans into individual paper cups for a special treat during the film. Nurse Eileen was unique and different from any other nurse I had encountered during my tenure in the hospital: she was gentle and genuinely kind, and I could tell she cared about her patients, even more so than Nurse Jack, who was also on my list of compassionate nurses.

As Nurse Eileen slowly handed out the cups of jellybeans, I noticed that she had a slight tremor in her hands. She handed me my thin paper cup full of the sugary treat, which I profusely thanked her for, although I had no intention of eating the jellybeans. I worried and began to obsess about the damage and havoc the sugar would wreak on my teeth, so I covertly placed my cup on the floor to my left. The next thing I knew, Tyrone's head swiveled around in response, as if he had invisible sugar receptors that could sense unattended treats, and he was instantly by my side. It happened so quickly that I was in a state of shock; I had no idea that Tyrone could move his gigantic girth so swiftly and quickly. Although in utter consternation at his speed and spriteliness, I had the foresight to turn my head away from Tyrone, and I fortuitously avoided having his exposed bottom in my face as he knelt on the floor and lifted my paper cup to his mouth, swallowing the entirety of my jelly-beans whole. After this, he rushed to the table behind me and emptied the remaining contents of the bag of jellybeans into his mouth before Nurse Eileen even knew what had happened. Tyrone was standing with his soiled hospital gown wide open in the back and trying to lick the plastic bag clean of any remains of sugar when Nurse Eileen finally made it over to him; she gently spoke to Tyrone, and whatever she said was inaudible to me, but it calmed him down immediately and once again, he plopped down on an empty plastic chair, ready for the start of the movie.

- EWWW! Everybody look! She's bleeding! YUCK!

Connie ran around the Day Room, shouting at the top of her lungs about some poor, unfortunate patient who happened to be bleeding. I quickly scanned the room - the group looked fine to me; in fact, everyone except me was intently focused on watching the movie and seemed to be enjoying themselves. There was only so much gear changing with Vin Diesel's bulging biceps and tire squealing that I could handle, and my attention wandered and wavered from the very start of the film.

- IS IT CONTAGIOUS?

Connie's voice was so incredibly loud that it felt like she was screaming directly into my ears; I turned around in my seat to find her standing behind me and pointing to my head with utter disgust.

- EWWWW! EWWW!

She cried and continued to point at me, like a toddler who had seen something distasteful, and it was then that I realized that I was the source of her repulsion. I touched the top of my head with my right index finger, and surprisingly, it was slightly wet. Upon closer examination, my finger was covered in dark, burgundy, wine-stained blood. I suddenly felt eight pairs of eyes staring at me as I flushed with embarrassment and shame; Connie's shrieking managed to pierce the concentration of my fellow movie watchers and seemed to rattle Nurse Eileen's usual calm demeanor. I tried to run out of the Day Room into the hallway, but the neuropathy in my feet put this plan to a screeching halt, and I was forced to drag myself slowly down the empty hallway and into the refuge of my room.

I sat on my carefully made bed sobbing with my head in my hands; I had not realized that I was picking the scab on my head again, as it was simply a nervous habit. Unfortunately, my lack of hair, combined with Connie's disgust, had caused this private habit to be made public and visible to the entirety of the Day Room. As I cried and dry heaved, I touched my head compulsively and realized that the scab was quite small, and the tiny amount of blood was already dry. My wound was already healing, and it was not anything serious to begin with. I tried to apply this logic and reason to the situation, but these attempts failed, and I was unable to calm myself down. Eventually, I wore myself out and curled up into a shape resembling the letter C, clutching and squeezing my pillow with my weak and tingly hands.

THIRTY-THREE

Nurse Eileen gently applied an antibiotic cream with gloved hands to the wound on my head as I sat on the edge of my bed with my head down so that I was in a good position for her to see the scab. When she finished, I lifted my stiff neck up, and we were face to face when a strange look came over Nurse Eileen's usually kind face, and I thought that she might cry.

- Why did you do this to your head, Deborah? It's because you want to harm yourself, isn't it?

I was taken aback by Nurse Eileen's semi-rhetorical questions and decided not to answer her, as she clearly had made up her mind regarding my scab-picking motives. She shook her head and tutted and looked at me with utter pity; in response, I felt frustration and anger fire in my entire body. I did not want or need anyone, including Nurse Eileen, to feel sorry for me or commiserate on my behalf; my pride was wounded, and I was at a loss as to how to respond and convey that self-harm was not the same thing as anxiously picking at a scab on my head, it was just a habit that I engaged in when stressed, like biting one's nails. If I really wanted to hurt myself in the way she implied, I could find much more dangerous and potentially life-ending manners of doing so. I rolled over on my bed and onto my left side and faced the wall that continuously emanated cold air, carefully waiting for Nurse Eileen to hobble out of my room.

THIRTY-FOUR

- I brought you some food. I know you've been having trouble eating.

My mouth watered, and my stomach gurgled in response to Aurelia's statement; I imagined that she brought me spicy green curry with chicken and jasmine rice from my favorite Thai restaurant, Thep Phanom. When Aurelia visited me in the past, Krishna and I had always taken her there for a meal; even she had to acquiesce and agree that it was the best Thai food that she had eaten in the United States.

Much to my chagrin, a Ziploc bag full of old and discolored nuts was slammed onto the dining room table in front of me.

- Here. Raw almonds. At first, I thought that Aurelia was joking, as her voice was almost robotic when she belligerently placed the almonds in front of me. I desperately waited for the punchline and my hearty meal, but when I looked up at Aurelia's deadpan face, I remembered that she did not possess a sense of humor. She was serious about my snack. I ignored my hunger pains and chose not to say anything to her, as I knew it would only turn her mood even more dour.

- This city is so dense – how do you stand it?

Internally, I was instantly defensive about my city and my home – I loved San Francisco. I wanted to pick a fight with Aurelia and ask her how she stood living in the middle of the desert in Arizona with only a 'guru' and a bunch of sad sycophants for company, but I willed myself to calm down and refused to give in and answer her question.

- We went for a walk in Japantown today, and that helped.

I could care less about where Aurelia walked earlier in the morning, but when she said *we*, my curiosity peaked, and I vaguely recalled Susan mentioning that Aurelia had a spiritual sidekick in town. I wondered who this mystery person from her community was and how she had manipulated him/her into believing she was the one in dire need of help. I pondered this as we sat in stony silence for what seemed like ages. I was in the middle of the table, and Aurelia sat next to me in the chair to my right; I was starting to feel enveloped in anxiety and claustrophobia, and I wished that she would sit across from me so that I could have some personal space. I could feel her anger emanating towards me at a rapid pace, and as I sneaked a look at her out of the corner of my eye, her tight jaw and furrowed brow confirmed the animosity I systemically sensed in my body and psyche. We continued to sit together at the table; the dining room was completely silent except for the noise my stomach made as it tightened and churned due to hunger and nerves.

Suddenly, Aurelia's chair creaked, and she craned her neck to the left with a fake smile on her face; her mood swiftly changed to that of overwhelming positivity, and she loudly proclaimed:

- I have news! Crystal just couldn't stay away! She just happened to be in Mt. Shasta and drove down to San Francisco to lend support.

I groaned internally as I realized that Crystal must be Aurelia's curious friend that Susan had mentioned. I felt ganged up upon, as I knew Crystal was not here to advocate on my behalf. Quite the opposite: I feared that her presence would guarantee that Aurelia would succeed in forcing me to stay in this institution – or somewhere worse - indefinitely.

Crystal was obviously hovering outside of the dining room and listening to our entire interaction, for as soon as her name was mentioned, she instantly walked into the room. Unfortunately for Aurelia, she did not look like a spiritual aid or rock of support: Crystal looked petrified and traumatized. I knew it was from simply being on the psych ward, as I had seen visitors with heartfelt intentions of supporting their loved ones in need, immediately stricken with shock and trepidation after being thrust into this new and unknown environment outside of their comfort zones. Although Crystal's motives for visiting me were questionable, she also fell victim to the magnitude of the hospital's atmosphere – smothering, bleak, and unsafe.

Crystal fumbled around the room as if she was drunk and finally sat down across the table, precisely in the middle of Aurelia and me, so that we formed a triangle across the large dining room table. It had been years since I had seen her at one of Aurelia's gatherings, and she had not aged well; she was now in her sixties, but the evidence of the early years of her life spent in the sun as an alcoholic and chain smoker was now visible on her leathery face, which was a map of past indiscretions: deep wrinkles formed ravines that split off from each other, only to converge again in new areas of her skin.

I recalled that Crystal often referred to her decades of addiction as her *past life*; her current incarnation began when she found her spiritual path via a tarot reading from a psychic that led her straight to the clutches of Bodhi. I also knew that she possessed a wicked sense of humor and could be incredibly sharp-witted and jovial; additionally, she was Aurelia's only friend who could have a conversation without proselytizing. Conversely, she could also be ungrounded and spacey. I willed that good-natured, funny side of her to appear, but when I looked at her, it was clear that she was not herself. Crystal had not acclimated to the hospital yet, and she sat at the table with incredible stillness. She looked like she had seen a ghost – pale, shaken, and wide-eyed. I sneaked a glance at Aurelia, who was furiously tapping her phone. *Is she playing a game?* I wondered. I squinted my eyes and willed my distance vision to work, and I was able to see a bunch of bright colors shaped like gumdrops moving frantically and exploding like fireworks across the tiny phone screen. Any offense I felt disappeared in an instant as I realized that I could potentially use her phone for one last plea for help to the outside world.

I continued to ignore Crystal sitting across the table like a stunned character out of a zombie apocalypse movie and I turned towards Aurelia and forced myself to use the nicest voice that I could muster, although it made me sick to my stomach to do so.

- Can I use your phone?

I sweetly asked this question and startled Aurelia, who was deeply engrossed in her game.

- Why?

Her retort was immediate and expected; I had my next line prepared.

- I want to text Dr. Gerrard. She's technically legally deaf and only responds to text messages.

- I didn't know that. Aurelia snapped.

- It's true. I implored her to believe me, for it was the truth, but I had forgotten this crucial detail about Dr. Gerrard until now.

Aurelia stopped playing her game and looked up at me while holding her phone protectively and at a good distance away from my reach.

- You can use the phone, but I'm not going to *enable* you.

The haughtiness of her tone made my skin crawl, and I wished that I could scream at the top of my lungs and vent all my frustrations; I also yearned to forcibly ask her to leave the dining room and, subsequently, my life. Instead of unleashing my pent-up grievances, I swallowed them in what seemed like a self-betrayal for one last chance of reaching Dr. Gerrard.

DR. GERRARD, *it's Debbie Hartung. Please help* – 911. *Text this number. I'm in the hospital, and I really need your help. Can you visit me? Thank you.*

I felt a huge sense of relief after I hit the green send button on Aurelia's phone; I let out the enormous breath I had been holding in, only to feel a sudden force on my right hand as Aurelia snatched her phone back.

THIRTY-FIVE

In the time it took for me to beg Aurelia for her phone and text Dr. Gerrard, Crystal acclimated to the psychiatric ward and reverted to being very loud and chatty. Her Boston accent boomed across the dining room and carried down the hallway; apparently, she was trying to convey a message to me through a convoluted story about one of her alcoholic brothers. It was impossible to tell which brother it was. I knew she was from a family of six siblings and that she was the only girl. Her family was originally from Ireland, and her parents emigrated to the USA in the 1950s, settling in South Boston, where her father was a hard-working fire-fighter. In addition to excelling at his job, he was also a master of spending his paycheck at the local pub and alternately impregnating and beating his wife, who took her angst out on her children.

- When Spirit told me that I had to cut him off – my own brother, I thought, youse guys must be kidding me!

As Crystal continued to babble about her brother, I tried to figure out how this monologue related to me while deciphering her Southie accent, which replaced the *R's* in her sentences with an *AH* sound and her *O's* with an *AW*.

The classic example of this being, *Pahk your cah in Hahvad Yahd.*

- He was living out of his car in a park somewhere, and the only money he had for food and gas was what I sent him each month. I meditated and prayed, and I finally did it. Oh, shit, I thought, he's gonna die. I wasn't wrong, but Spirit had a plan. It was the dead of winter – the kind of cold that will just freeze your balls right off. Anyways, he drove into town for some liquor and collapsed at a package store. He ended up in the hospital, and the doctors did a bunch of tests and discovered that he had pancreatic cancer. I went and visited him and noticed that his nurse, Mary, was taking very good care of him if you know what I mean. Anyways, he gets discharged and moves in with her! I can't make this shit up; I swear! Mary takes care of him for a year, and they fall in love. Then they get married right before he transitions over to the other side.

Aurelia appeared to be listening to Crystal's tale, but I saw her glancing down and using her phone quite frequently, and it was clear that she was not internalizing anything her friend of many years was saying. Something was afoot with Aurelia, and I had a sinking feeling in the pit of my stomach. *She's probably deleting Dr. Gerrard's messages.* In that instant, I knew that I had no hope of reaching Dr. Gerrard as Aurelia continued to do everything in her power to block me from potential freedom. My glimmer of hope amidst this darkness was Krishna: he would be home in three days, and then everything would be alright. I knew that he would rescue me and take me home where I could rest and recuperate.

Just as I was thinking about Krishna, Crystal finished her tale, and I decided that it was just nervous ramblings and did not relate to my situation in the slightest. As if reading my mind, Aurelia turned to me with a bizarre look on her face.

- You don't know what's going to happen with Krishna. He may not want to continue your relationship. He's on a very special journey right now and is collecting soul fragments. His vibration is here (she raised her right hand above her head), and yours is here (she touched her hand on the grimy hospital carpet).

I took a deep breath in, and my eyes searched Aurelia's face for some kind of remorse. *What is she saying? Krishna is going to break up with me?* My mind spun, and I felt sick to my stomach as I turned my back on Aurelia and, subsequently, Crystal in disgust. I faced the dining room window covered in dirt and condensation from the non-stop rain. I did not move a muscle until I heard Aurelia and Crystal leave the room.

THIRTY-SIX

- Who knows who Georgia O'Keefe's husband was? I will give you a hint: he was also an artist.

Nurse Eileen opened a large, hardcover book of O'Keefe's paintings; she expertly turned to a black and white photograph of the painter's husband. As soon as Nurse Eileen asked this question, my hand flew up, and I wanted to answer her immediately. She sat on a chair with her back towards the window, encircled by her mentally ill ducklings. Nurse Eileen nodded to me encouragingly, and I felt safe to proceed; as if I were in preschool, I wanted to outshine my fellow pupils by answering the teacher first. This proved to be an easy task as my fellow preschool students were tired and bored; most of their eyes were glazed over, and spittle was starting to creep down the sides of their mouths, and they dreamed of nap time.

- Alfred St –

Shit! His surname was on the tip of my tongue. I knew he was a photographer and a bit older than Georgia, but I could not conjure up his name, no matter how hard I tried. I dropped my head into my right hand and rubbed my temples in frustration and defeat.

- You were so close, Deborah! Alfred Stieglitz. *Of course*. Nurse Eileen looked at me approvingly, and my ego felt slightly less bruised.

- Let's back up a bit. Has anybody heard of Alfred Stieglitz before tonight?

Nurse Eileen's question was completely ignored by everyone in the circle, including me. I thought it was preposterous to be asking a group of sleepy and distracted psych ward patients – a few of whom had begun rocking in their chairs - about a photographer that most art students might not be aware of. I folded my arms over my chest and yawned; I was exhausted as well, and all I wanted was my bed, never mind how uncomfortable and foul-smelling it was. *How did I get roped into Psych Ward Art History Class anyway?* I had no idea what time it was, but the dark, starless night sky indicated that it was getting late. Now I remembered: I was on my way to take my evening dose of Trazadone, dragging my tingling feet down the hall at a rapid pace when I passed the Day Room. I was almost in the clear when I heard Nurse Eileen calling my name; I reluctantly turned around, and she immediately shouted to me from the Day Room to join the circle for the evening's entertainment. There was something pleading in her eyes and a slight twinkle as if to say; *I did this for you.* I exhaled loudly, walked into the Day Room, and took my place in the circle, as I knew that she had gone to great lengths for me. I was too tired to show the gratitude that I felt in my heart, but I hoped that she could sense it.

- O'KEEFE BEGAN CREATING simplified images of natural things, such as leaves, flowers, and rocks. These are two of her paintings from that time, both entitled *Red Canna*.

The early portion of her mid-life was a blur, but I became cognizant again just in time to learn about Georgia O'Keefe's flower paintings from 1920 -1922. Nurse Eileen opened her coffee table book to show us the paintings; she slowly went around the circle, holding the book still so that each patient could get a good look at O'Keefe's work. Once again, psychiatric ward preschool began, and I noticed that some of my fellow patients showed a flicker of interest in story hour and viewing the paintings, which looked to me like close-ups of bright red, flowering vaginas. I found Story-time comforting, and I liked being read to by Nurse Eileen. I took a few deep breaths and felt my body melt into my uncomfortable plastic chair in relaxation as Nurse Eileen carried on about O'Keefe's paintings of New York's skyscrapers and skylines.

THIRTY-SEVEN

Jamie was curled up in her bed across from me, and I could tell that she was still awake. Emboldened by our bonding session during Candy Land, I decided to ask her a question. *The question* that had been on my mind since I first encountered her. I could not fight my medical curiosity anymore: *What was her diagnosis? Why was she here? Undiagnosed bipolar disorder?* Jamie was obviously not suffering from psychosis or overtly depressed. I never saw her look anxious or have major mood swings; I would have known by now if she heard voices. I also noticed that she was not forced to take medication like the rest of us.

- Who put you here?

I asked amidst the great void of darkness in our room.

- Me?

Jamie questioned and seemed slightly annoyed at the boldness of my inquisition; in truth, it surprised me as well, but I continued.

- Were you in the hospital or –

- My brother and his girlfriend put me here, but they forced me to go to the emergency room first.

I lay in my bed silently as I could sense a possibility that Jamie might open up to me.

- Apparently, I had an anger episode, and they were scared, so here I am.

I was scared, too, as I recalled that Jamie was a kindergarten teacher. *What if she has an episode while teaching?* Her tone was one of understandable frustration with her situation, but she was not hostile in the slightest towards me. Before I could pry her for more information, she announced that she was tired and turned over in her bed quite forcefully, effectively ending our conversation.

THIRTY-EIGHT

- Deborah! Deb-o-rah! Wake up!

I groaned in my sleep; even with my eyes closed, I sensed the obnoxiously bright hallway light, and I knew the door to my room was open. I was confused and still half-asleep, but I knew that someone was calling my name; I fought, drifting off again into a deep sleep, and turned over on my left side. I was taken aback; Nurse Eileen was standing directly over me, smiling and grasping something very tightly in her hands.

- I brought you a present! Before her generosity could register in my foggy brain, she excitedly shoved two objects into my hands.

- I read in your chart that you like to write. Here! Maybe this will help pass the time.

I could see that Nurse Eileen looked conflicted: she seemed excited, yet she kept looking over her shoulder furtively. I assumed that she was afraid that the other nurses might see her giving me a present. I was instantly wide awake when I realized that she had placed a miniature note-book and a golf pencil into my hands.

- Don't tell anyone about the pencil; you're not

supposed to have anything sharp. I smiled and held onto the pencil and notebook with dear life; I also noticed that the pins and needles feeling in my hands had returned. I vigorously rubbed the sleep from my eyes and looked up to properly thank Nurse Eileen, only to discover that she was gone.

THIRTY-NINE

I sensed it was early morning, and Jamie's bed was empty. Her standard, hospital-issued sheet and blanket strewn wildly across it confirmed my intuition. Her bath towel remained folded and unused on her nightstand. Gloom encased our room, even with the overhead light on and the glaringly bright hallway light. The wind whipped around frantically outside the window, and the rain came down in heavy, loud droplets, creating a hissing sound as they hit the sullied windowpane. *PSS, PSS, PSS, PSS!*

I used all my strength to force my eyes to focus, and I grabbed the mini golf pencil and blank notebook that Nurse Eileen had given me from my drawer. I wanted to thank her for her kindness, but I knew that her shift was long over; I sensed that putting her presents to use would suffice. I gripped the tiny pencil, ignoring the pain and tingling in my right hand, and began scribbling on the first blank page of the miniature notebook. I let my frustration, sadness, guilt, grief, and shame swirl in my brain for a moment, and then I put my emotions to paper. Miraculously, my hand wrote quickly and efficiently as I purged my deep sorrows. I allowed myself to cry, and thick, salty teardrops welled up in my eyes and then dripped down the side of my face; I was too engrossed in my writing to wipe them away, and they eventually dripped off my jawbone and created wet spots on the paper. I filled the first ten pages of the notebook with a basic timeline of what happened, my guilt and self-blame, and the immense betrayals that I felt, especially from Aurelia. Eventually, when I was spent, I felt lighter and clearer from my writing exercise. I hid my pencil back in my nightstand drawer and began reading what I wrote. When I looked down at the pages before me, I thought my eyes were deceiving me: the dramatic, emotion-laden prose that I spent an hour writing was nowhere to be seen. In their place were the illegible scribblings of a toddler. I sobbed and heaved: my brain and right hand had also betrayed me.

FORTY

The band inflating around my arm was like a balloon being blown up as it squeezed my left tricep tightly; I was half asleep, but I instantly felt wide awake from the intense pressure around my arm: it was like an espresso shot for my entire body. Just when I thought it was finished, the pressure increased again as it gripped my upper arm. My face grimaced in response until the machine beeped to indicate that my blood pressure had officially been taken; the suffocating air around my right arm was quickly let out and made a high-pitched squeaky sound.

- You're all set! I studied the unusually chipper nurse to the left side of my bed, and I wondered why she brought the vitals machine into my room instead of leaving it in the dining room. As she fiddled about with multiple sets of cords, I could see very pristine and new colored tattoos on her forearms: a hook and anchor, a mermaid and a pirate ship battled for attention while her stretched earlobes shimmered underneath the overhead lights with drusy plugs.

- Oh! I forgot to introduce myself to you. I'm Sierra! I'm a student nurse at a nearby hospital, and I will be here this morning.

Sierra politely omitted that this was her mandatory psychiatric ward round, but I could sense it. She stopped trying to tame the cords of the blood pressure machine and turned and faced me; she put her hands on the hips of her very tight black jeans and tilted her head and Bettie Page style haircut towards me; her cat-eye shaped glasses were slightly slipping down her nose, and her light brown eyes were almost hidden by thick, jet black, winged eyeliner. Sierra smiled at me and bared a set of perfectly white, cosmetically straightened teeth. The large grin on her face said *I'm the nurse that's going to save the world – including you!*

FORTY-ONE

The Day Room was teeming with student nurses – each one more upbeat than the last. The group of ten mid-to-late twenty-year-old female nurses sitting at the table in the Day Room looked up from their phones in unison and smiled at me when I walked into the room. They beamed with youth, vitality, and freshness, unscathed by the stressors of real-world nursing. Additionally, each one was wearing a lot of makeup for 9 in the morning, and not one hipster hair was out of place. Fresh and expensive colored tattoos graced their thin forearms. One of them boomed: *Welcome!* I visibly cringed and started to turn my body closer to the hallway as I was already plotting my exit.

- Sit down! We brought the paper for you to read. Bettie Page half encouraged and half ordered me to join the table; I turned my head to see where my fellow patients were, as I knew the newspaper was not technically only for my enjoyment. Only Roger, the foul-smelling old man, was in the room in disheveled street clothes, which reeked of rotting cabbage. As usual, he was on the couch and watching the Weather Channel on the television, which was once again showing a stagnant weekly forecast of storm clouds and rain.

A nurse quickly stood up from the table to make room for me, and I knew that my fate was sealed: I would have to join the table. I felt uncomfortable and intimidated, but I forced myself to sit down on the rickety plastic chair being offered. A head nod was all I could manage for a 'thanks.' I grabbed the closest section of the newspaper, which happened to be the crossword section of the *San Francisco Chronicle*. Vertical and horizontal lines of empty, numbered boxes crossed and confused me; I squinted, but I could not read the clues no matter how hard I tried. I was frustrated and let out a loud sigh, which was unheard by the student nurses, who were engrossed in drinking coffee from thermoses and mason jars and gossiping and giggling quite loudly about the goings on – some boring and some sundry – at school.

I turned the paper over and skimmed a recipe for *Quick and Easy Paella* (*Paella de Mariscos*), but I was never a fish lover, and the raw ingredients began to turn my stomach. I sighed quite audibly this time, in increasing frustration and agitation; I picked at the cuticles on my nail beds until they bled. I quickly lost interest in the newspaper, and my thoughts suddenly turned dark; I began to ruminate. Something Aurelia said during her visit last night was stuck in my head on repeat: *His vibration is here* (*hands overhead*), *and yours is here* (*hands on floor*). *What if Krishna breaks up with me? What if I have ruined everything?*

I felt a crushing sensation in my chest, and tears welled up in my eyes when I imagined the worst with Krishna; once again, I was beaten down and broken.

FORTY-TWO

Cranky Nurse brusquely informed me that I had two visitors enter the hospital and that they were in the process of going through the metal detector and security check before being permitted to see me. She pointed to an abandoned intake room and gestured for me to enter and wait for my visitors. I waited and waited, and still no visitors. *What's taking so long?* As a distraction, I looked around at my sparse surroundings: an old, clunky computer on a wheeled monitor stand, three empty plastic chairs, and one twin bed. I avoided the bed at all costs and sat down in the chair closest to the hallway. The sole window in the room was covered in molecules of condensation that dripped onto the floor; heavy pellets of rain belted down outside, and the sky looked gray and ashen.

I could tell by the heavy footsteps in the hallway and the *SWOOSH!* sound of sopping wet rain gear that my visitors were not Aurelia and Crystal. I breathed a sigh of relief for a second, but then my thoughts turned to the fear of the unknown: *Who's visiting me? Why now?* I was lost in my thoughts and staring at the grime-covered window when I heard the brisque sound of footsteps approaching me; I turned my head to the open door of the intake room and was greeted by two smiling and familiar faces: Thomas and Herschell. The bright light emanating from the hallway juxtaposed the somber lighting of the intake room, giving them halos for a fleeting instant. I was so relieved to see my friends standing before me that I barely noticed how soaked they were from head to toe. Thomas removed his black raincoat to reveal a fabulous black cape underneath and looked at me with a twinkle in his eye and a slight grin on his face.

- We ran into your aunt in the security check. She was with her *friend*. You didn't tell me that your aunt was a lesbian!

- She's not a lesbian; she just has a bad haircut.

My response to Thomas's assumption about Aurelia's sexuality was so quick-witted, unexpected, and deadpan that it even shocked me. Silence hung in the air afterwards and Thomas looked at me, then turned his head to the left and looked at Herschell. Then, two sets of eyes stared at me, and in unison, my friends proceeded to laugh and giggle uncontrollably. I relaxed for a minute after hearing the laughter of two of my fellow artists and dearest friends; it brought me back from the horrible landscape of my psyche where I was once again under Aurelia's influence: where I was guilty, paranoid and convinced that I had done something so terrible that Krishna would end our relationship upon his return from India.

Thomas launched into a story about his first boyfriend when he was a teenager in Los Angeles; somehow the tale related to the downpour of rain outside and possibly my hospitalization, but I could not follow the plot. Instead, I began to curl up on my chair and felt myself breaking down: I was raw with emotion, fear and guilt and there was nothing that anyone could do to soothe my nerves.

- Then I tried calling you, but a nurse said that you were busy.

I looked up at Thomas in consternation; his dark brown skin was still wet with rain droplets, and they were very close to falling into his brown eyes, with especially white sclera's, and onto the shoulders of his crocheted black cape, which I knew Herschell had made for him.

- Then I tried again every fifteen minutes, and the phone was either busy or there was no answer.

Herschell turned in his seat to face me; his blueish green eyes matched the color of his teal t-shirt, and he sported glasses and a thin, silver ponytail from the rim of hair on the bottom half of his head. Always empathetic and caring, he was waiting for the right opportunity to simply ask how I was doing.

- And how are you?

His gentle manner combined with the adoration I could feel from Thomas was too much for me and I burst into tears and began to dry heave and rock in my chair.

- I'm so sorry. I'm so sorry. What have I done?

My thoughts were scattered, and the voice of fear pounded and reverberated in my consciousness; I couldn't help but speak them aloud.

- I should have called you; that would have been the solution. Then I wouldn't be here. What have I done? I'm sorry.

I was inconsolable and traumatized, but my friends tried their best to comfort me and gently bring me back to reality.

- What is this place?

I looked up at Thomas, who was sitting in front of me on a rickety, old plastic chair, and Herschell, who had taken a seat to my left. They exchanged glances, and it seemed like they had an entire conversation in one look, as couples often do; it was decided that Herschell would answer my query.

- It's a kind of holding ground and stabilizing part of the hospital. The goal here is to get you back on your medication as quickly as possible and then turn you out onto the streets again so that someone else in need can have your bed. You will not get in-depth healing here.

If what Herschell said was true, and it did make perfect sense to me, why was I being held here indefinitely if someone else needed my bed? I saw other patients come and go, yet I was not allowed to leave.

- When I did outreach work for Hospitality House, across from General Hospital, we used to have a lot of clients who had just been released from their psych ward.

I looked at Thomas as he continued to speak, and I shivered; the psychiatric unit at General Hospital was rumored to be rough, dirty, and full of intensely ill souls, much worse than where I found myself.

Eventually, Thomas and Herschell had to leave – they had to take two buses to get back to their apartment – and I felt my stomach tighten and drop in their absence, which was profound.

PART 3

There Is a Light That Never Goes Out

Take me out tonight
Take me anywhere, I don't care
I don't care, I don't care
And in the darkened underpass
I thought, "Oh God, my chance has come at
*   last"*
But then a strange fear gripped me
And I just couldn't ask
Take me out tonight
Oh, take me anywhere, I don't care
I don't care, I don't care

And if a double-decker bus
Crashes into us
To die by your side
Is such a heavenly way to die

And if a ten ton truck
Kills the both of us
To die by your side
Well, the pleasure, the privilege is mine
Oh, there is a light and it never goes out

THE SMITHS

FORTY-THREE

Cranky Nurse was visibly annoyed that I had another visitor about to enter the psychiatric ward – it meant more work for her. I was pondering the phrase she used to describe this mysterious being: *He has a funny accent.* I pondered what kind of accent could be humorous or strange to her ears as I stood like a trained puppy at the Nurses' Station behind the half-door that separated me from the world at large; I waited for my visitor to make himself visible.

My ears perked up before I saw his face, and I stood frozen in consternation, tears already streaming down my face. *It can't be him, can it? That was his voice!* Before I had time to worry about my appearance or feel any of the shame that Aurelia berated me with, my heart leaped and jumped in my chest – this time not from fear but from excitement. I saw his thin figure turn the corner from the security check into the hallway of the hospital; he sported his standard-issue grey drainpipe jeans, black Converse sneakers, a black button-down shirt, and a worn-in, black leather jacket. There was a new, rich, caramel-brown hue to his skin from the Indian sun, and his short, black hair was growing out and starting to curl at the ends. When Krishna looked at me, his large green-brown eyes immediately locked with my eyes, and I felt his intense stare exude compassion. Like something out of the romantic comedy movies that I despised, the next moments happened in slow motion, and I felt a spinning sensation as an invisible camera panned outward as Cranky Nurse finally opened the barrier for Krishna to walk through, but first, she demanded possession of the miniature porcelain Ganesha painted in bold, bright shades of magenta, orange, blue and red that he brought me from his travels. The next thing that I knew, he hugged me with all his strength, and I collapsed and sobbed in his arms; Krishna kissed my face sweetly and wiped away my tears. When I apologized over and over again and asked for forgiveness, he firmly stated, *There's nothing to forgive.* Then Krishna hugged me again and kissed me on the lips. I knew at that moment that our bond was not severed or broken; it was stronger than ever.

Unbeknownst to me, Connie was circling around us like a shark who sniffed blood as the entire hospital watched our reunion; the only thing missing was clapping and fireworks. When Krishna's embrace finally let go, and he grabbed my hand, we felt Cranky Nurse's eyes bore into ours as she silently demanded an explanation for the happiness and love on display in a psychiatric ward that she did her best to keep somber and terrifying.

- We haven't seen each other in a long time.

This was all Krishna offered Cranky Nurse in way of a response, and when Connie incessantly asked me if this was my boyfriend, I happily nodded my head with the knowledge that Krishna was that – and so much more.

FORTY-FOUR

I was almost jumping out of my seat with excitement, and I could not concentrate on the occupational therapy happening in the Day Room. Ten minutes prior to this, I was accosted in the hallway by a hospital employee unknown to me: she was short and stocky, with a head of frizzy and curly brown hair; her glasses were thick and magnified her eyes so much so that she looked like a lemur wearing tons of mascara. Apparently, she was a social worker, and she popped out of a door behind the nurses' station. When she left the door open by mistake, I saw a wall of computer monitors with small figures scurrying back and forth. *They've been filming and watching me the entire time.* Somehow, this did not surprise me.

- Deborah, now that your boyfriend is back, we have decided to release you tomorrow on the condition that you attend a mandatory outpatient program to address your depression for at least two months.

- Yes! I will attend any outpatient program that you want. The words flew out of my mouth quickly, and if my feet were not eighty percent numb, I would have been tempted to jump up and down in anticipation of my impending release. First, Krishna made his triumphant return yesterday, and now this, things were really looking up.

Ms. Lemur blinked a few times and stared at me with a puzzled look on her face. I wondered what was so strange about my reaction. She prattled on about the outpatient program, which, coincidentally, I was already enrolled in, thanks to her foresight. I was given very specific instructions and guidelines about the outpatient clinic; finally, Ms. Lemur handed me the stacks of official yellow papers with typed directions to the clinic and all of her notes. I tried my best to concentrate, but her eyes were huge at this point, and I couldn't stop staring at the clumps of thickly applied mascara that moved up and down as she blinked incessantly. I scribbled my initials on a pink piece of paper, which was challenging as my hand was throbbing and tingling; then Ms. Lemur disappeared behind the secret door again, and I was left feeling elated in the middle of the hallway. *FREEDOM!* I could hardly believe it; my head spun, and I felt as if I might float away with happiness.

I tried again to focus on the task at hand: filling out another useless occupational therapy worksheet entitled *Coat of Arms*. The white sheet of paper had an empty shield haphazardly drawn on it with six boxes that relate to my personal credo. I was so relieved to be leaving the hospital; it was impossible to give any attention to this assignment, so I scribbled the first, mostly banal, answers that came to mind.

Name: *Debbie*
Comfort Food: *Ice Cream*
Person You Admire: *MLK*
A Proud Moment: ?
Goal for the Week: *Stop Negative Thoughts*

.   .   .

I LOOKED around the large table in the dining room and suddenly realized that Tyrone was sitting extremely close to me and leering at my chest; automatically, I hunched forward and tried to cover my breasts with my crossed arms. His worksheet was filled with childlike scribbles, nothing legible in sight. Connie and Tiffany Number One were absent from the activity, of course, as they point blank refused to participate in any organized activities. Lauren was across the table from me, scribbling away on her worksheet, as was Alex. Aaron had emerged from his room again and looked to be focusing as well, though it was hard to tell how much he really understood with his faraway stare, bloodshot eyes, and saucer-like pupils. My bet was that he suffered from psychosis, and these were all side effects from some very strong medications. Jaclyn sat a few seats away from me, and she was still sporting her booty shorts, a tank top, and flip-flops; she was impervious to the freezing cold temperature of the psychiatric ward. The final participant in OT therapy for the day was Tiffany Number Two; she was easy to spot, as her track marks covering her skinny forearms revealed a recent history of IV drug use; she also had stringy, dirty strawberry blonde hair and yellow teeth. She looked to be in her late forties, and her orange wristband was sealed tightly around her wrist, alerting the staff to the potential danger she possessed.

I did not pay the slightest attention to the Occupational Therapist, but I could not help but notice that she had a high-pitched, squeaky voice. I let my mind wander, and random thoughts floated in and out of my consciousness: *I can't wait to take an Epsom salt bath when I get home. A cup of Krishna's chai will taste so good.*

The Occupational Therapist asked Tiffany Number Two

to share her proud moment from her crest, and she talked about going on methadone and trying to get clean; I was only half listening though, and I really could not stop thinking about the many things I would do – and eat - upon my release from the hospital. During my daydreaming, a new worksheet silently appeared in front of me: *Discharge Planning*. I quickly scribbled my answers on the photocopied piece of paper.

Goals I have set for myself before leaving the hospital:
Pack.
Mentally Prepare.

Information I need to know before discharge and the person I need to talk to:
Dr. Mueller?

What level of care has been recommended to me for the next step? In what way will this treatment be useful?
Outpatient therapy to help address depression.

Who is part of my support network?
Dr. Gerrard.

What practical problems do I need to plan for transportation, taking medication, and finding a pharmacy?
?

What steps can I take to avoid rehospitalization in the future?
Greater self-awareness.
Get help sooner.

I quickly scanned my answers to the questions at hand,

and I was a bit surprised to find that I thought that I needed to pack before I left the unit, as my belongings were under lock and key, and I was mentally ready to leave the hospital the minute I arrived.

I WAS SITTING in a conference room near the dining room, and I was quite comfortably curled up cat-like in an oversized round, faux suede chair; the only things on my mind were my impending release and getting back to my life with Krishna. I gave up trying to pay attention to Sharma Patel, a licensed social worker, who was desperately trying to lead most of the patients in group therapy on the unit. The task was simple: state what brought you to the hospital and what could be done in the future to avoid rehospitalization, but even that seemed taxing to me. I just tried my best to relax and avoid being called on, mostly by averting Sharma's intense gaze.

- Alex, let's start with you. Sharma nodded encouragingly to Alex, who was sitting still and had refrained from pacing the halls for the last ten minutes.

Alex compulsively stroked his chin and looked down at the floor; his right leg went TAP, TAP, TAP! along to an internal rhythm. He pulled at his sturdy hospital bracelet after he was finished touching his chin.

- I, I guess they said I should wear a medical alert bracelet because doctors get confused and always want to hospitalize me.

- I take it this isn't your first hospitalization, Alex? Sharma was gentle but prodding. Alex shook his head No. My ears pricked up, and I began to pay attention to the conversation; I was constantly curious and diagnosing other patients in my head, but I could not grasp Alex's illness. I waited patiently for a clue.

- I was in another hospital before this, and the doctors agreed that if they couldn't figure out what was wrong with me, they were going to put me in a state facility. I shivered and felt sick as I thought of what occurred in state facilities. If this city-run psychiatric hospital felt like *One Flew Over the Cuckoo's Nest* to me, a state-run facility would be a book in the horror genre. Alex was silent and averted his eyes from Sharma's; she asked him three times what his diagnosis was, but he refused to answer her. I arched my back against my chair, and I also avoided calling attention to myself; luckily, my tactics worked, and Jaclyn was called upon next.

- I moved out here from L.A. to be homeless with my Mom. I left my kids with my Auntie, and I have been living in a tent downtown for a month or so. Anyway, I'm here because I hear voices and the other day, they told me to run into traffic South of Market. I was almost killed, and I'm... I'm worried I won't be able to get my kids back.

I held my breath as I waited for Sharma's response to Jaclyn's revealing share. It appeared that Lauren was also holding her breath across the room from me, while Alex stared off into outer space and Tyrone sat next to him with a diminished smile. Roger reeked as usual, and I could tell that he still had not bathed or washed his street clothes; he had a look of indifference on his face. A new patient sat next to Sharma, a young Asian boy who looked just shy of being an adult; he wore an Urban High School sweatshirt and had an air of entitlement that I found strange. Just as Sharma opened her mouth to finally respond to Jaclyn, she was interrupted by Tiffany Number One, who sat at the head of the circle, next to Jaclyn. Tiffany Number Two was nowhere to be seen; I presumed she was in her room resting.

- Girl, don't you worry about the kids. Ima fighter and

me and my kids, we'll come down to L.A. with you for a while and live with you. We'll help you get your kids back, too.

While Tiffany Number One continued to rave about the amazing presence that she and her kids would have in Jaclyn's life, I felt sick again. Neither Jaclyn nor Tiffany Number One could take care of themselves, let alone children. I feared for their kids.

Yes! That will be great. You can stay at my house, and it will be so FUN!

Jaclyn was instantly best friends with Tiffany Number One and while they loudly plotted and schemed many upcoming adventures in L.A., Sharma completely lost control of the group therapy session. Tiffany Number One and Jaclyn won possession of our therapy session and as they continued to laugh, giggle and hug each other wildly, the rest of the group, including me, recoiled in their seats and tried to block them out.

FORTY-FIVE

Krishna and I begged and pleaded with Dr. Mueller to release me a day early; he kept staring at Krishna in disbelief, as if he was surprised that he existed and that I had not hallucinated him. I doubt that he heard any of our arguments supporting an early release.

- The paperwork is already completed for tomorrow – you will be fine for one more night here. Dr. Mueller was firm in his answer and was clearly annoyed that we had now switched to begging for a release.

- Is there a way that you can just change the date of the paperwork, please? I made the request as nicely as possible, while Krishna nodded his head in agreement.

- No. If it bothers you that much, speak to the public defender. Dr. Mueller motioned to a disheveled man in an old suit standing a few feet behind me; I assumed he was a new patient only minutes before.

I turned to face Krishna while Dr. Mueller walked away from us.

- It can't hurt – just talk to the public defender. We've got to get you out of here today, if possible. I nodded my head in acquiescence, but internally, I was scared to speak to the public defender.

- I have to go back to work now, unfortunately. I will see you later tonight and hopefully, we can go home. Krishna looked at me with his large brown eyes and squeezed my hand, trying to give me a boost of confidence to speak to the public defender, as he must have sensed my nervousness.

I APPROACHED the public defender and introduced myself; he did not follow suit and immediately got down to business, though he was distracted and constantly looking at his phone.

- What are you in here for? I was taken aback for a second by his question, but I forced myself to be honest and direct.

- A suicide attempt.

- Hmmm... the hearing is in less than an hour and I have a lot of patients to represent today. If it was a cry for help, I can help you. If you did something stupid, like take pills, you're on your own. The court meets every Monday, maybe I can help you next week.

I was shocked by his candor and that he called me – and my situation in general – *stupid*, as that was not the adjective that first sprung to my mind. *How rude!* I turned around in a huff and skulked back to my room, knowing that I was stuck on the psychiatric ward for another twenty-four hours.

FORTY-SIX

- We've tried to visit you a few times in the last twenty-four hours, but Krishna has always been here. You're not allowed more than three visitors at a time, so we've had to leave.

This confused me as I knew that three visitors were allowed at once. I saw through Aurelia at once, and I knew that she was avoiding Krishna on purpose, as there was no way that he would stand for her behavior and manipulations.

Aurelia was clearly annoyed that Krishna was spending all his free time since returning home from India with me, but I was not affected by her negativity and was not bothered in the slightest that she and Crystal were inconvenienced. *Only a day to go until my liberation!*

- Well, now that I've finally got you alone, we need to talk about the details of your release. I know I said earlier in the week that I would stay as long as needed and help you transition back to your life outside the hospital, but that's not going to work for me anymore. I'm leaving tomorrow night.

Aurelia stared at me with her small, blue eyes, which blazed with fury. I instantly moved my chair further back from her and silently counted my blessings that she was leaving and that I had not heard her the first time when she offered to stay in San Francisco indefinitely.

- That's fine with me. I left my answer at that, not wanting Aurelia to change her mind and stay in San Francisco.

- What do you need for your release? I can't find your phone charger anywhere...I have your phone...how are you getting home?

While Aurelia bombarded me with questions and the minutiae of my departure from the hospital, I noticed Crystal sitting across from me with a pensive look on her face.

- Are you listening to me? Aurelia had her gander up, but once again, I was not flustered by her attitude.

- I am. I don't need much. Krishna & I will take the bus home or call a cab.

- Fine. That's fine with me. I guess I can call you a Lyft if worse comes to worse. What else do you need? Are you sure that you don't need your cell phone charger?

- A pair of sunglasses, perhaps? I joked while looking out of the dining room window and taking in another rainy, dreary day.

- Where are they? What do they look like? I was confused for a minute, and then I realized that Aurelia did not pick up on sarcasm in general, so I just answered her questions in the hopes that we could change the topic of conversation soon.

- They're white Ray-Bans, and they are on the top of the dresser in my bedroom.

While Aurelia was taking notes on her phone regarding the whereabouts of my sunglasses, Crystal started questioning me about my friends, Thomas and Herschell.

- How do you know them? Crystal had asked with a bit

of a strange look on her face. I was unclear as to why this information was necessary, but I curtly answered her questions.

- Krishna and Thomas worked together at Marcello's Pizza in the Castro almost thirty years ago, and they've been friends for a long time.

- But what about Herschell? How does he come into the picture?

- What do you mean? I questioned back, unsure of her line of thought, though I had a sad hunch where it was going.

- How do Thomas and Herschell know each other?

- They're married. I hoped my short answer cleared up her misunderstanding and naiveté, but the barrage of questions continued.

- Which one is Herschell?

- What? I knew what Crystal was implying, and I was not interested in her line of questioning at all. I made this very clear by the tone of my voice and body language, but she insisted on continuing.

- What are you really asking? I demanded.

- What, what, I mean is...which one is the black one? Herschell, right?

I turned my head away from her with intense anger and bit my tongue, refusing to answer her utterly rude and ignorant question. Not to mention that racist ignoramuses always assumed that Herschell was black; he and Thomas had been dealing with these bizarre assumptions their entire relationship, which spanned decades. I was sick and frustrated and finished with Aurelia and Crystal; I stood up and walked out of the room as quickly as my tingling feet could carry me.

FORTY-SEVEN

- Deb-o-rah! Time to wake up! Deb-o-rah!

I rolled over onto my left side and saw a new nurse with a huge smile on her face like a cheshire cat; she beamed at me while I rubbed my eyes and tried to force myself awake. It was then that I realized today was the day: my freedom awaited.

- Can I go home now? I quickly asked, although it was probably only 7:30 in the morning.

- Slow down, honey. I need to take your vitals first and then we can talk. I'm Karen, by the way.

I stared at her cherubic face and pale, white skin, which was exaggerated by bright pink lipstick and brown hair with thick, blonde highlights. She had tiny crease lines around her brown eyes, which were incredibly kind. I decided the least that I could do was follow suit and introduce myself as well. Also, I was secretly hoping that she would have information about my impending release.

- Nice to meet you. I'm Debbie, I stammered.

- Oh! I thought you were a 'Deborah.'

- I am, but no one has ever called me that...except here.

- Well, it's nice to meet you, Debbie. Can I have your arm? I need to take your vitals now.

I stretched out my left arm, and while Nurse Karen fiddled with the Velcro strap and pressed random buttons on the vitals machine, I noticed that she was staring at me intermittently. I self-consciously touched my right hand to my head, thinking that she must be staring at my lack of hair or the scab on top of my head. The armband on my left arm began to inflate and constrict my tricep.

- I just have to tell you, honey, that you're really very pretty. I don't know what you're here for. I just returned from a vacation, and I haven't had time to read your chart, but I can tell that you're very smart, too. Look at your porcelain white skin and bright, green eyes. You don't need makeup at all! How many women can say that?! Nurse Karen continued to praise my appearance, and I felt instantly embarrassed, and my cheeks flushed in response to her compliments. In truth, I had not thought about what I looked like in over a year, and I had avoided looking into the mirror the entire time that I was on the psychiatric ward for fear of seeing the ghost of my former self staring back at me.

- Thank you. It was all I could muster in the moment, and although I wanted to ignore her compliments entirely, I knew that that would be rude, so I forced myself to be gracious.

- Do you know when I will be able to leave?

I asked the burning question, hoping with every fiber of my being that she could give me a definitive time for my departure.

- Hmmm...let me see here. I don't see anything about a time written down, but then again, I just got back from vacation. Patients are usually allowed to leave just before lunch. But then again, I don't even know what you're in here for.

Nurse Karen looked at me with quizzical eyes and raised eyebrows; I felt compelled to share a synopsis of my story with her, as she seemed so caring. However, after I told her about my attempted suicide – leaving out the details of the New Age cult to save time – she looked at me strangely, and something dark took over her demeanor.

- You really ought to be grateful that you're not in jail. It's illegal to try to take your life in some countries. My mouth hung open in consternation; I could not believe that she would say something so cruel after complimenting me only minutes before. Nurse Karen clearly was not the kind soul I thought she was. I ended our interaction by turning my body away from her and facing the wall, after which she quickly left my room.

I was glad to be alone again, and I quickly put Nurse Karen's comments out of my mind. I looked around the room and found Jamie's bed empty and unmade once again. A large, white plastic bag that read Patient's Belongings in thick, blue ink had appeared on my bedside table. It took me thirty seconds to pack, and then I made my way to the doorway; I paused for a second and then walked out of the room on tingling toes, making my way down the hallway for my final hospital meal.

FORTY-EIGHT

I was unsure of myself and my newfound freedom. I assumed that I would be jumping for joy and bubbling over with excitement and conversation after being released from the psychiatric ward, yet something cautious and strange had taken over my being. I was completely silent, and I felt confused and lethargic: in just seven days of being held against my will in the hospital, I had forgotten how to behave in the outside world. Krishna met my concerned stare, gave me a nod of encouragement, and reached out to grab my hand. Just as our fingers were about to touch, an object of cold plastic was thrust into my outstretched hand.

- Here. I couldn't find the sunglasses you said were on your dresser, so I bought these at Walgreens for you.

Aurelia's announcement seemed odd to me, as I recalled that my sunglasses comment was sarcastic, for it rained the entire length of my stay and no sunshine was ever seen. I also quickly realized that there was no way that Aurelia would have dared enter my apartment with Krishna home, so her comment about not being able to find my sunglasses was just another one of her lies.

I stood on the stoop of the hospital, somewhat stunned

for a few seconds, and then, for the first time in almost a week, I let myself deeply inhale air from the outside world. As my lungs expanded and I took in large gulps of fresh air, my entire body seemed to slowly awaken from a deep slumber. I looked beyond my immediate surroundings and saw that just beyond the building's stoop, which was covered in dark shade, the sun was indeed shining. This seemed like a good omen; I mumbled a *thanks* for the sunglasses and put them on top of my head, ready for my descent down the steps of the hospital and into the warm sunshine.

The sun blazed down on me, and although it was only sixty degrees out, I felt its power warm me to my core. I basked in the sun and turned to look down the steep street, trying to orient myself to my new surroundings while simultaneously enjoying the topography of the city I loved. Krishna was in no rush to move and stood patiently by my side; he sensed that this was an important moment for me. As I looked down the steep hill, I saw Aurelia move out of my peripheral vision. She was moving at such a fast pace that it seemed like her heels never really touched the ground.

- Where are you going? Don't you want to go out to lunch with us? As soon as the words flew out of my mouth, I was full of regret. *How could I be polite to someone who was so cruel and twisted? Aurelia was responsible, at least in part, for the past seven days of my living nightmare.* The answer came to me quickly: I was hardwired to be nice, no matter what the cost, which caused me intense frustration. This sensation was short-lived, however, as Aurelia yelled back at me while continuing to furiously move down the hill, and my attention was diverted.

- I'M DONE! I booked you an Uber; what more do you want? I need some alone time; I've extended too much. I'm going to the movies, and then I'm on the first flight home. I can't do THIS! Her hands gesticulated wildly, and she continued to rant and rave even when she was out of earshot. I watched her march down the hill, and the goddess on the back of her shirt seemed to be staring back at me; I shuddered. Aurelia continued to move her hands wildly in the air and was still yelling and talking to herself, even at the base of the hill. My eyes widened, and I turned to look at Krishna; in that moment, I knew we shared the same exact thought: *She looks like a mental patient.*

- Let's hope that's the last we ever see of her. Krishna spoke first, and as I stood there watching a tiny figure in the distance behave like a mad woman, I had never agreed with him more.

KRISHNA OPENED the back door to the Uber and held the door open for me; I motioned for him to get in first as I quickly turned my head and stared at the building across the street. It was unassuming, with brown brick and a street address absent from the naked eye; it was calmly perched on top of a hill in San Francisco's Mission neighborhood. It looked completely harmless from the outside, yet I knew it would take years for the trauma of the building's interior to completely escape my system.

I finally climbed into the black Toyota Prius and immediately noticed that the large, swarthy man in the driver's seat was eyeing my standard-issue, plastic hospital belongings bag with suspicion. I removed it from the leather seat and placed it gently on the floor as the car began to move. Krishna stared straight ahead to avoid motion sickness, and as the car began to quickly drive down the steep hill, he gently placed his hand in mine, giving it a squeeze. I smiled. It felt strange to feel my face move in this manner, as it had been almost a year since my lips curved upward and inner happiness outwardly expressed itself. I let my eyes wander, and I was soon looking out of the window with a soft gaze; I opened the window and let the cool air wash over my face, deeply inhaling the faint eucalyptus scent of San Francisco that I had loved since I first arrived in the city at the tender age of eighteen.

AFTERWORD

I was one of the lucky ones. Sadly, many lives are lost each year due to suicide. Although I initially wrote this book for my own healing, I'm sharing it not only to shed light on the stigmas surrounding mental illness but also so that those suffering may find hope. Your life matters. You matter. If you or someone you care about is struggling, dial 988 or 911 immediately; help is available. Also, there are additional resources below.

It took me seven years to write *The Factory of Maladies* because my experience was so intense; while writing, I also processed the PTSD I was experiencing as a result of my hospitalization. I wanted to give up many times because of the triggering nature of my project, but deep down, I knew that if I completed my memoir, it would be the ultimate catharsis. After I finished the book and read it in full, I realized that it had the potential to help demystify the preconceived notions around mental illness and also that it might give a fellow sufferer hope and comfort and alleviate feelings of alienation.

In addition to writing, painting also helped me heal on many levels (www.debbiehartungart.com). I would be remiss if I did not acknowledge the supportive and kind therapists and doctors at UCSF's Langley-Porter Outpatient Clinic; they gave me the tools to once again function on a daily basis.

RESOURCES

988 Suicide and Crisis Lifeline: 988 or Lifeline Chat
Crisis Text Line: Text HOME TO 741741
NAMI – National Alliance on Mental Illness: www.nami.org (mental health programs)
CDC – www.cdc.gov/suicide/facts/index.html
National Institute of Mental Health –www.nimh.nih.gov/health/topics/suicide-prevention
2020 Mom –www.2020mom.org (policy, training, resources)

Reasons to Live **by Juliana Bruno** - This book is a great resource for anyone suffering from mental illness, and it's also a wonderful tool for friends & family of anyone suffering from suicidal ideation.

Suicide Prevention and Awareness
Save.org
988lifeline.org (national hotline)

ACKNOWLEDGMENTS

I have an overwhelming number of people to thank and feel grateful for. First and foremost, I feel very grateful to the individuals who were with me in the hospital; I hope that you received the care, help, and compassion that you deserve. Thank you for sharing your journey with me. I would also like to thank the kind nurses and staff that I encountered during my tenure on the psychiatric ward.

Also, an enormous 'thank you' to Susan George and the mysterious police officer who saved my life; gratitude does not even come close to explaining how I feel. To Krishna for being by my side and always believing in me, especially my creativity. I would be remiss if I did not thank my parents for cheering me up after I was released from the hospital and for encouraging my writing since I was a child. A giant dose of gratitude goes out to Alicia Cobb for truly being the best of friends while I was in the hospital and for helping with my recovery after I was released. This book would not be here if MB, Tara Bhat, Conor Henry, and Steve Brown had not encouraged me to keep writing no matter what; also, for their edits, proofreading, and support from day one.

Thank you to Stephanie Roberts Hartung for reading an early draft of this book and for giving such insightful comments. Thank you to Thomas and Herschell for visiting me in the hospital and for being such loyal friends.

I would also like to thank the following people for their support and friendship: Kimberly Davis, Surya Bhat, Danna Carballo, Kate Langlois, Jaya Bhat, & Kelly Elmore.

A big 'thank you' goes out to my fellow Pisceans, Brenda Knight and Duncan MacLeod, for their friendship, encouragement and publishing insight and wizardry. Last but not least, I send gratitude to Mike T. for creating the beautiful pen that I used to edit and write early drafts of this manuscript.